Illustrator:
Jose Tapia
Larry Bauer

Editor:
Janet Cain, M.Ed.

Editorial Project Manager:
Ina Massler Levin, M.A.

Editor-in-Chief:
Sharon Coan, M.S. Ed.

Art Director:
Elayne Roberts

Cover Artist:
Sue Fullam

Product Manager:
Phil Garcia

Imaging:
Hillary Merriman

Publishers:
Rachelle Cracchiolo, M.S. Ed.
Mary Dupuy Smith, M.S. Ed.

Early Childhood Units
for
DRAMA

W9-CKJ-489

Author:

Lynn DiDominicis

Teacher Created Materials, Inc.
P.O. Box 1040
Huntington Beach, CA 92647
ISBN-1-55734-207-9

©1995 Teacher Created Materials, Inc.   Made in U.S.A.

Table of Contents

Table Of Contents (cont.)

Introduction

There are many opportunities for oral expression in the classroom. Students enjoy taking part in activities that allow them to express themselves in a creative way. Learning is fun and takes place in an environment that promotes fluency, comprehension, and increased socialization.

There are many techniques that can be used in oral expression. Generally, they fall in the categories of oral language organization and oral interpretation.

Oral Language Organizers

Before oral interpretation takes place, have students organize the facts of the story. This can be done with the whole class or in cooperative learning groups. Techniques include the following:

Summarizing the Story

Students tell what happened in the story, in proper order, using their own words.

Plot and Character Analysis

Students examine the problem in the story and tell how the problem is resolved. They can also look at the physical and personality traits of the characters. The characters in one story can be compared/contrasted with those in other stories.

Story Mapping

Using a grid, students follow the progression of a story from beginning to end.

Retelling the Story

Students retell the story in their own words, usually with the teacher writing the information on the chalkboard. Use a three-column chart such as the one shown below. This is an effective way to help beginning readers recognize words.

beginning	middle	end

Brainstorming Ideas and Background

Students share ideas. All ideas are accepted equally.

Pocket Chart Activities

Sentence strips are used to build word recognition, sentence structure, and sequence of ideas.

Venn Diagram

This is a diagram that shows differences and similarities. Two characters or stories can be compared to see how they are alike and how they are different.

Introduction *(cont.)*

Oral Interpretation

There are many ways to express what a story is about. Students increase their comprehension of a story when they recreate it in their own way. Examples:

Choral Speaking

Give the explanation part of the story to a narrator. Choose one group to do action or repeated parts. Place that group in the middle of the stage, giving students some movement to perform. Give the remaining parts to other groups, placing those groups at different places on the stage.

Rapping

A narrator tells the basic plot of the story in rhythm, with the class repeating key phrases using the same rhythm. Use snapping fingers, clapping, and rhythm band instruments.

Singing

If you prefer not to sing, you can use tapes, records, or CDs. You can also tape record someone, such as a musician, playing the piano or your students singing.

Readers' Theater

This is a wonderful way to use drama in your classroom because students do not have to memorize a script. For very young students, simple stories can be memorized. No props or costumes are used, so add interest by placing your readers at different levels, some standing, some sitting on chairs, and some on the floor. Give narrator and action parts to different students.

Creative Dramatics

Students retell the story through action. Help them with dialogue and costumes.

Puppetry

Puppets are a great way to dramatize a story and promote comprehension and socialization skills.

Mime

Retelling a story using mime can help comprehension without the burden of reading.

Pageantry

Assign parts and present a stage performance. Everyone takes part in completing the play. It is done grandly, with lots of action, scenery, props, and costuming.

Themed-Program Performance

Sometimes a program is done around a theme, such as "Bears," rather than using a specific book. Then, original stories, poems, and songs are used to present the theme.

The ideas listed above can easily be used in the classroom or as a stage performance. This book will explain these techniques in detail and provide suggestions for using them.

Introduction (cont.)

Organizing Drama in Your Classroom

Once you begin to have students participate in drama activities, there will be many things you will want to keep on hand and store. Many of the things you make or collect can be reused. After you have organized your drama materials by themes or stories, they will be easily accessed when you need them. Some ideas to get you started are shown below and on page 7.

Scripts

Scripts can be reused if you make them to last. Make as many copies as you need, plus a few extra. Glue copies to cardboard or manila folders and laminate them. When you are finished using them, store them in a big envelope or manila folder and label them. Scripts should always be taped to the inside of a puppet stage for the puppeteers to follow. Use picture symbols instead of words for very young students.

Puppets

Any handmade stick puppets or paper bag puppets, etc., should be saved as a resource for puppet presentations. Puppets can easily be stored in labeled shoe boxes.

Puppet Stages

There are many kinds of puppet stages that work well in the classroom.

Curtain Rod and Sheet. From a hardware store, get a curtain rod or wooden dowel rod that is 6 feet (1.8 m) long. Hem one end of a twin-size flat sheet and put it on the rod. Hang the rod over two chairs or anywhere that is convenient. This type of stage can be constructed quickly and is easy to store.

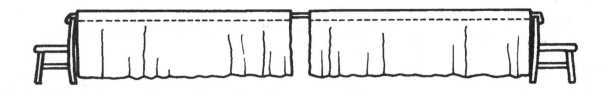

Large Cardboard Carton. Obtain an appliance cardboard box from a store, cut a hole in the front, and decorate. This type of stage is fun to use but can be difficult to store.

Science Presentation Board. Buy a tri-fold science presentation board from any teacher resource store. Cut a square in the upper half of the board's middle section. Place with the two sides going towards the back. Then decorate with paper or paint. You will actually be using the wrong side of the board. This type of stage folds up and can be easily stored.

Introduction (cont.)

Tapes

Many dramatic performances are enhanced by the use of prerecorded tapes. Tapes can be made of the actual script, background music, or background noises. Be sure to save these tapes by labeling them and storing them in the box with the appropriate play.

Lighting

Lighting is important in drama production for stage and classroom presentations. Lights add interest and emphasis to a performance. This can be done fairly simply in the classroom.

Overhead Spotlight. This is done by making a hole in the middle of a black piece of construction paper and taping it to a piece of clear or colored transparency. Tape the construction paper and transparency to a transparency frame. Place it on an overhead projector. Use a clear transparency and a small hole to create a spotlight effect. Use a colored transparency and a large hole to light the stage.

Stage Lights. Buy two metal workroom bulb frames with clip-on tongs from the hardware store. Put two colored spotlights in them. Then clip them to the back of two chairs, pointed at the stage. You may want to plug them into a power strip so that your lines are grounded. Do not use more than three spotlights per outlet.

Black Light. This can be very dramatic and effectively used with a board puppet stage. Black light strips can be purchased at any lighting store.

Transparencies

Backgrounds can be created by drawing scenes with watercolor markers on a transparency. Then use an overhead projector to project the background onto a wall, a piece of butcher paper, or any plain background. Be sure to put the projector on the floor and shine it at an angle. Otherwise, the actor will interfere with the image.

Props

You will find yourself collecting many props as you use more drama in your classroom. Much time and effort will be saved if you keep these props. Cardboard storage boxes can be used for bigger items. Shoe boxes and big envelopes are an excellent way to store smaller items. Stools can be used for performances, such as choral speaking, rapping, and readers' theater. Try to get some of these donated. It does not matter if they match.

Background Scenery

If you use painted flats for the background scenery in large productions, find a place to store these in your school. These can be painted over from year to year. Invite the art specialist at your school to get involved in these projects.

Performance Ideas

WHO WILL COME TO SEE OUR PERFORMANCE?

- Parents and other family members
- Members of the community
- Another class
- A high school language arts class
- A college education class
- Residents from a retirement or nursing home

WHAT WILL WE PRESENT?

- A puppet show
- A play
- A collection of drama activities
- A theme presentation: Bears, Candy, Community Workers, Fairy Tales, Animals, Holiday Program

WHERE WILL WE PRESENT OUR SHOW?

- On the school stage
- In our classroom
- In a church
- At the library (school or public)
- At a shopping mall
- At a retirement or nursing home
- In someone's backyard
- At a special community event
- In a high school or college classroom
- At a daycare center

WHEN WILL WE PRESENT OUR SHOW?

- During the school day
- After school
- On a Friday or Saturday evening
- On a weekend morning or afternoon
- During a PTA meeting

Invitation

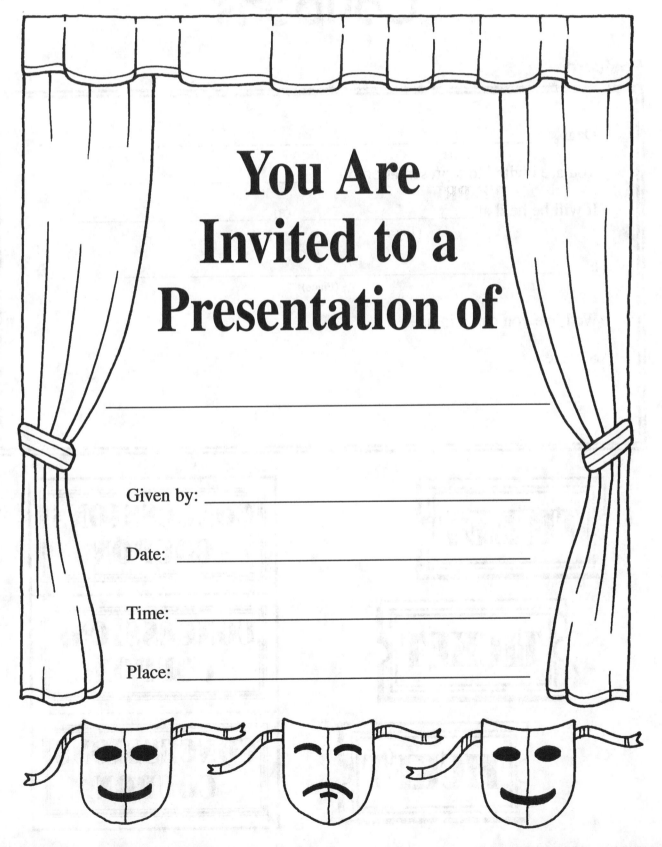

You Are
Invited to a
Presentation of

_____

Given by: _____

Date: _____

Time: _____

Place: _____

Postcard, Tickets, and Coupons

Postcard

Dear _____,

You are invited to a presentation of _____.

It will be held at _____ on _____
                            (Time)   (Date)

at _____.
                                      (Place)

We hope you can join us.

Sincerely,

_____

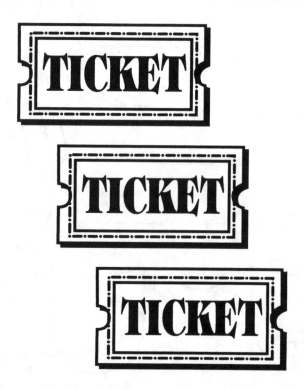

Goodie Bag Decorations

Directions: Reproduce, cut out, and color the goodie bag decorations. Staple them to paper lunch bags and fill with popcorn or candy.

The Teddy Bear's Picnic

by Jimmy Kennedy

Summary

The words to a children's song are used as the text of this book. The events that take place at the teddy bear's picnic are described.

Extension Activities

Teddy Bear's Backyard Picnic Party

This idea can be used for a Saturday morning party in someone's backyard. It can also easily be adapted for use on the school playground during the week. The party should last a couple of hours. Suggestions for how to organize the party are suggested below. The foods served should be simple. Lunch does not need to be included.

Invitations: Make bear-shaped invitations (page 15), and send them home with students. Collect some extra teddy bears in case some students forget theirs.

Food:

1. Make a teddy bear cake using the directions provided (page 16) or using a professional mold. Molds are available from Wilton Cake Pans which are sold at most department stores, or they can be ordered directly from Wilton Enterprises at 1-708-963-7100.

2. Ask some parent volunteers to make teddy bear-shaped cookies or purchase some at the store.

3. You may also wish to have parents make traditional crisped rice and marshmallow squares. Call them "honey cakes."

4. If you are serving lunch, decorate small paper bags with the outline of the bear you used for the invitations. Fill each bag with a sandwich, chips, some carrot sticks, and some teddy bear-shaped cookies.

5. Serve apple juice and call it "honey juice."

Favors: Prior to the party, make or have students make teddy bear hats (page 17). Give students their hats when they arrive at the party.

Extension Activities *(cont.)*

Teddy Bear's Backyard Picnic Party *(cont.)*

Activities: Use some or all of the activities described below and on page 14.

1. This activity should be done at school before the party. Reproduce the Teddy Bear's Baby Book form (page 19). Help students fill out this form. Have them color covers for their books (page 18). Assemble a class book that includes each student's cover and form. Reproduce the class book so that there is one for every student in your class. You may wish to give these books as party favors.

2. Using a piece of butcher paper that is about 7 feet (2.1 m) long, draw a teddy bear in an outdoor setting. Cut a hole where the face should be, as shown in the diagram below. Color or paint the drawing. Hang the butcher paper from a clothesline, or attach it to pieces of cardboard that are taped together. Make sure the bear's face is no more than 3 feet (0.9 m) off the ground. Take photographs of students with their heads through the hole.

3. Present the marionette puppet play, Another Version of Goldilocks and the Three Bears! (pages 36-39), as entertainment for the other guests at the party. In place of the suggested overhead projector background scenery, paint a background scene on butcher paper. If possible, videotape the performance and replay it in class for students.

4. If possible, rent a bear costume or ask a volunteer to make one. Have someone come to the party dressed in the bear costume and read a bear story. See the bibliography (page 143) for suggestions. If you cannot find or make a bear costume, have someone dress up as Goldilocks, wear a teddy bear T-shirt, or put on a football uniform and come as a Chicago Bear.

Extension Activities *(cont.)*

Teddy Bear's Backyard Picnic Party *(cont.)*

5. Have students dramatize the story *Bear Hunt* by Anthony Browne (Doubleday, 1990).

6. Play "Pin the Belly Button on the Bear." Use the bear picture that you made for taking photographs. Obtain large buttons or use laminated construction paper circles as "belly buttons." Give each student a "belly button" with double-sided tape on the back. Blindfold students, one at a time, and have them put the "belly button" on the bear.

7. Have a "Most Wonderful Teddy Bear Contest." Some students may not wish to enter their bears in the contest. Allow students who do want to participate time to tell about their teddy bears. Then have all students vote to see which bear they think is the most wonderful. Display the results of the vote on a chart tablet and create a bar graph using the data from the vote.

Color Bears

Reproduce the Color Bears (page 20) for students. Have students color the bears using the appropriate colors. This activity helps reinforce color and color word recognition. You may wish to have students work with partners to play Concentration. Have partners cut out and combine their sets of Color Bears. Show them how to play the game by matching the colors of the bears.

Real Bears

If possible, take a field trip to a nearby zoo to have students observe real bears. Otherwise, show some videos about real bears. Ask students to compare/contrast different kinds of bears, such as black bears, grizzly bears, and polar bears.

Class Teddy Bear

Have a large teddy bear for the class that is purchased or made by a parent volunteer. Allow students to use the bear during creative play.

Bear Counters

Have students use bear counters (Teacher Created Materials #L725) as math manipulatives.

Picnic Invitation

You are invited to

Teddy Bear's Backyard Picnic Party

at _____
(address)

on _____.
(date and time)

Please bring your
favorite teddy bear.

Teddy Bear Cake

Use the following directions to make a cake shaped like a teddy bear.

Note: Be sure to ask parents whether their children have any food allergies or dietary restrictions.

Use aluminum foil to cover a piece of cardboard that is 4 feet x 2 feet (1.2 m x 0.6 m). Make two yellow cake mixes, using the directions on the box. Bake in four round cake pans. After the cakes have baked, allow them to cool. Then cut and arrange the cakes on the cardboard, using the diagram shown below.

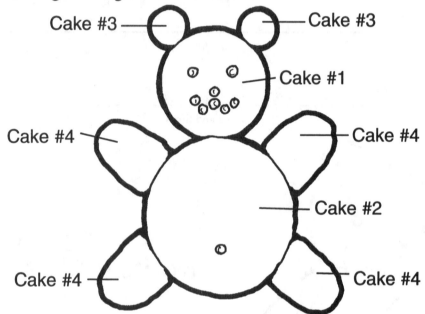

Cut around the edge of Cake #1 so that it is slightly smaller than Cake #2.

Use the top of a large glass to cut the ears out of Cake #3.

Cut the paws and feet from Cake #4 as shown here.

Use frosting or whipped cream to cover the entire cake. Then, decorate using gum drops.

Teddy Bear Hat

Teddy Bear's Baby Book

18

Teddy Bear's Baby Book *(cont.)*

```
┌─────────────────────────────────┐
│                                 │
│    (Paste photo or drawing here.)│
│                                 │
│                                 │
│                                 │
│                                 │
│                                 │
│                                 │
├─────────────────────────────────┤
│      Picture of My Teddy Bear    │
└─────────────────────────────────┘
```

Name: _____

Belongs to: _____

Height: _____

Weight: _____

Birthday: _____

Favorite Food: _____

Why my teddy bear is special: _____

_____

Paw Print

Color Bears

Directions: Color the bears.

If You Give a Mouse a Cookie

by Laura Joffe Numeroff

Summary

If you give a mouse a cookie, he will never be satisfied and will want all sorts of things to go with it.

 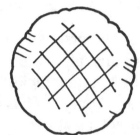  

Extension Activities

Mouse Mask

Have students make mouse masks (page 23) to wear when rereading or role-playing the story.

Bake Cookies

On the chalkboard, list some types of cookies, such as chocolate chip, oatmeal raisin, sugar, and peanut butter. Have students vote to see which type of cookie is the most popular. You may wish to use the data from the vote to create a graph. Then, locate a recipe that tells how to make the most popular type of cookie. Help students learn about baking and kitchen safety rules by making the cookies. Note: Be sure to ask parents if their children have any food allergies or dietary restrictions before using this activity.

Counting Cards

Reproduce the Counting Cards (pages 24-28) so that you have a set for each student, plus a set for yourself. You may also wish to make a set of transparencies colored with water color markers. Cut, color (using the specified colors), and laminate the cards. Then use some or all of the activities suggested below and on page 22.

1. Have students put the cards in numerical order. Then read them together in order.

2. Hold up your cards, one at a time, in random order. Have students find and hold up the corresponding card. Do this until all the cards have been shown. This improves color and number recognition.

3. Ask students to find the red card. Have them name other red things in the classroom. To improve color recognition and discrimination, continue with other colors on the cards.

Extension Activities *(cont.)*

Counting Cards *(cont.)*

4. Choose a math manipulative, such as bean counters or color tiles. Give each student, or each pair of students, ten counters. Hold up any card. Have students find the corresponding card from their sets. Then have them count out and place that number of counters on the card. Check to be sure they have the correct number of counters. This activity will help students understand number relationships.

5. Have students play a game with partners. The first partner picks a card and shows it to the second partner. The second partner then picks the correct card from his/her pile. For a more challenging game, the first partner picks a card without looking at it. The second partner gives clues, such as "Your card has four blue objects. What is it?" The first partner must give the correct answer from memory.

Story in a Bag

Encourage parents to send props for this activity (page 30). Tell the story "If You Give a Math Teacher a Present" (page 31) first using the counting cards (pages 24-28) and then using props in a bag (page 29).

Mice

Take students to the school library. Show them how to look for and check out nonfiction books that are about mice. Help students learn more about mice by reading aloud some of these books. If possible, keep some mice in a cage in your classroom. Allow students to observe the animals.

Irregular Plurals

Write the words *mouse* and *mice* on the chalkboard. Explain to students that *mouse* is used when there is only one and *mice* is used when there two or more. Provide additional examples of irregular plurals, such as *child, children* and *tooth, teeth.*

Mouse Art

Have students locate rocks that have shapes similar to mice. Allow them to use a variety of materials to glue features on the rocks, making them look more like mice. Examples include using yarn for the tails and felt for the ears.

Mouse Mask

Use the following directions to make a mouse mask. Have an adult help you.

Materials:

- paper plate
- scissors
- hole puncher
- string
- white, black, and pink construction paper
- tape
- stapler
- pipe cleaners
- glue
- black marker

Directions:

1. Use the scissors to cut two holes in the paper plate. These will be eye holes. Hold the paper plate up to your face to be sure you can see out the eye holes.

2. Punch a hole in each side of the plate and tie a piece of string to each hole.

3. Make a nose by cutting a semicircle out of white construction paper and rolling it into a cone. Staple the overlapping ends so the cone will stay together. Use strips of tape to connect the cone to the plate.

4. Make whiskers by gluing three pipe cleaners under the point of the nose. Allow the glue to dry. Cut a small pink circle and glue it onto the tip of the nose.

5. Cut two ears from white construction paper. Make the ears large and round. Staple them onto the top of the paper plate.

6. Use the marker to draw a mouth.

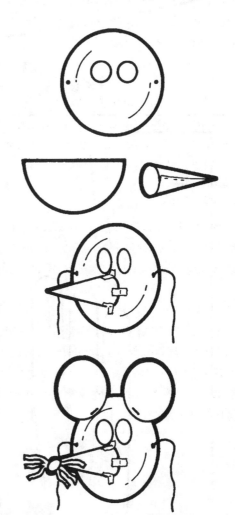

Counting Cards

1

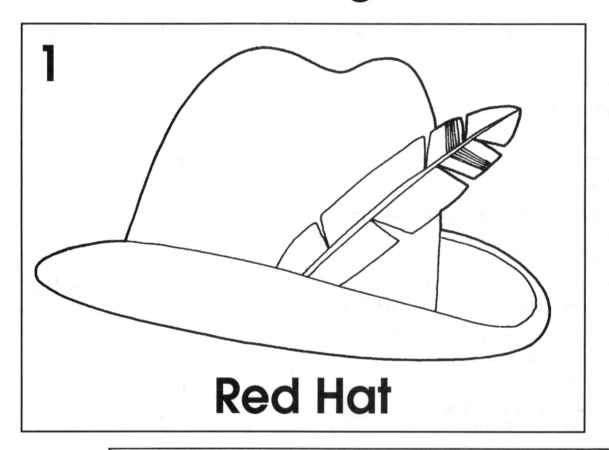

Red Hat

2

Green Gloves

24

Counting Cards (cont.)

3

Yellow Ribbons

4

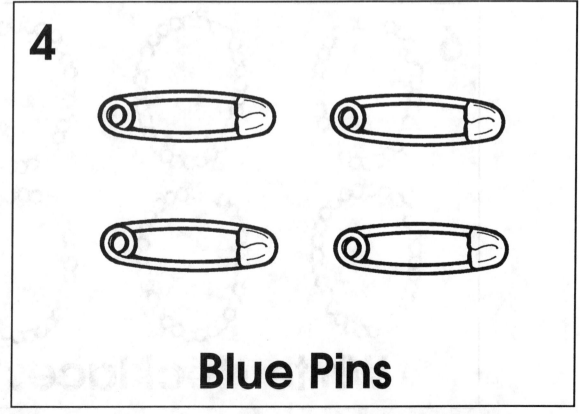

Blue Pins

Counting Cards *(cont.)*

5

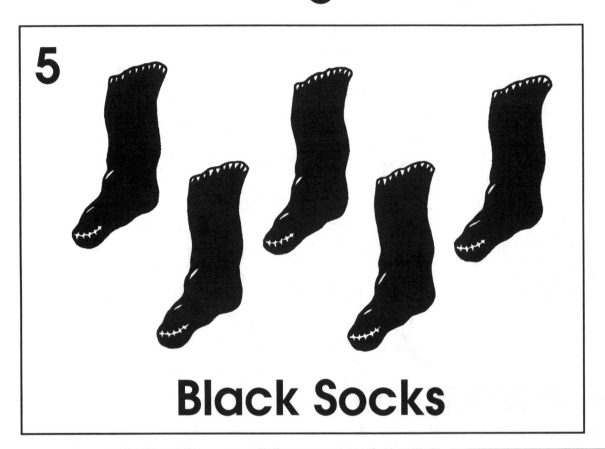

Black Socks

6

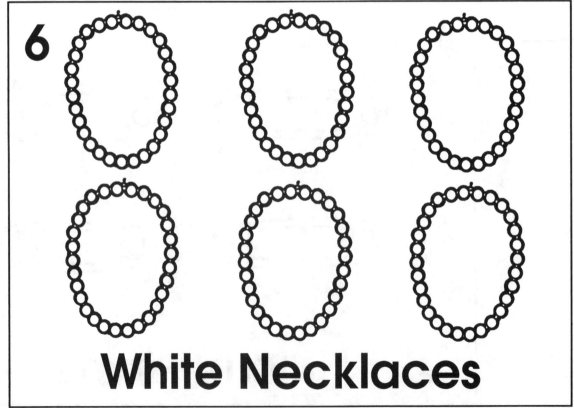

White Necklaces

26

Counting Cards (cont.)

7

Orange Flowers

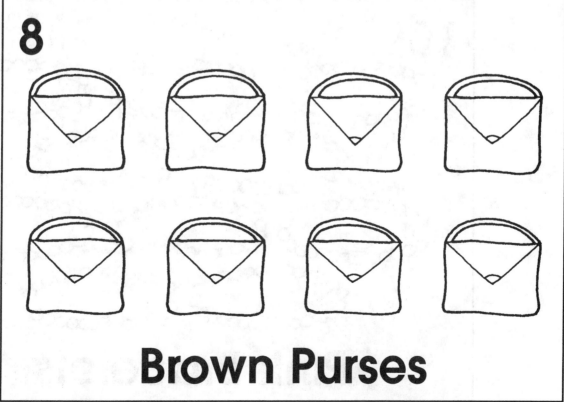

8

Brown Purses

Counting Cards *(cont.)*

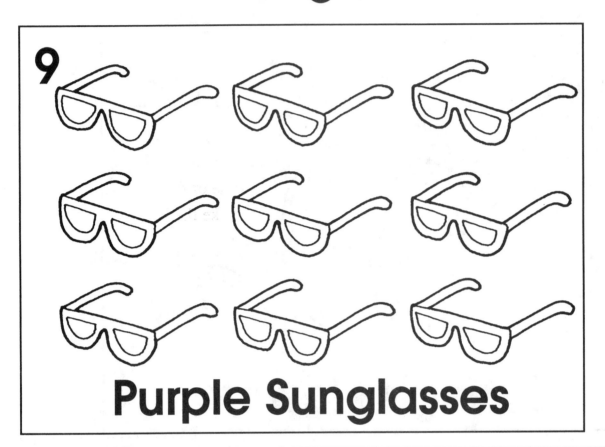

9

Purple Sunglasses

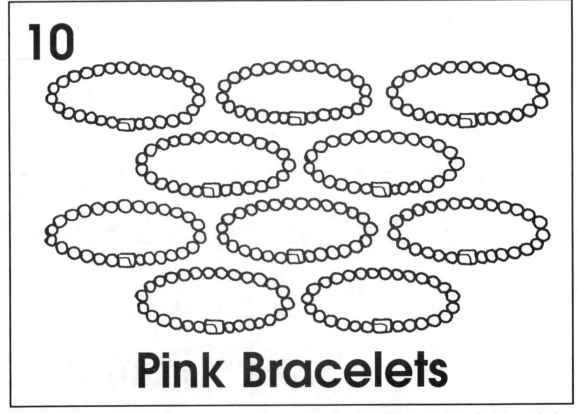

10

Pink Bracelets

Story in a Bag

If You Give a Math Teacher a Present

Materials: This will take some ingenuity and perseverance. Each type of prop needs to be gathered in the proper number and put in a bag.

Some suggestions for gathering props:

- Send home a note to parents (page 30), asking them to donate props.
- Find a local specialty toy company. They may sell some of these items in bulk.
- Using the Counting Cards (pages 24–28) as models, make the items you need out of construction paper, poster board, or cardboard.
- Once you have gathered these items, they can be saved, stored, and used from year to year.

Props you will need:

1 large cloth bag (a large pillow case may be substituted)

1 red hat

2 green gloves

3 yellow bows

4 blue pins

5 black socks

6 white necklaces

7 orange flowers

8 brown purses

9 purple sunglasses

10 pink bracelets

Directions:

Tell the story the first time using the Counting Cards (pages 24–28) as visuals.

Tell the story the second time using the props in the bag. As you tell each verse, find the proper items in the bag and put them on. You can put the items anywhere on your body. This should create a lot of laughter. When you get to the last verse, walk around the classroom, removing all of the items that are on you and placing them on students.

Parent Letter

Dear Parents,

We are getting ready for a special telling of the story *If You Give a Mouse a Cookie*. We are in need of some props and hope you can help. If you can donate any of the items listed below, please send them to school with your child by

_____ .

Thank you,

_____

 Teacher

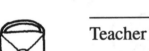

- Red hat   • Green gloves

- Yellow bows   • Blue (safety) pins

- Black socks   • White necklaces

- Orange flowers   • Brown purses

- Purple sunglasses   • Pink bracelets

If You Give a Math Teacher a Present

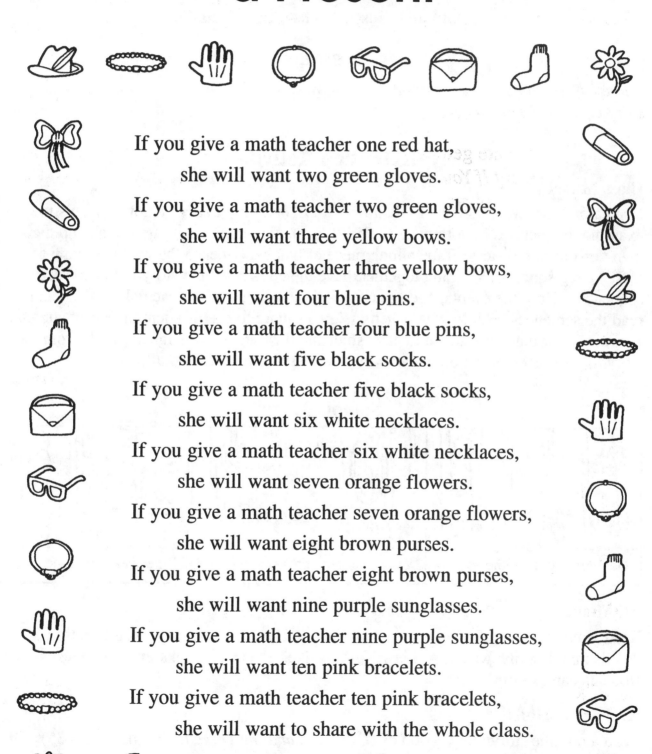

If you give a math teacher one red hat,
    she will want two green gloves.
If you give a math teacher two green gloves,
    she will want three yellow bows.
If you give a math teacher three yellow bows,
    she will want four blue pins.
If you give a math teacher four blue pins,
    she will want five black socks.
If you give a math teacher five black socks,
    she will want six white necklaces.
If you give a math teacher six white necklaces,
    she will want seven orange flowers.
If you give a math teacher seven orange flowers,
    she will want eight brown purses.
If you give a math teacher eight brown purses,
    she will want nine purple sunglasses.
If you give a math teacher nine purple sunglasses,
    she will want ten pink bracelets.
If you give a math teacher ten pink bracelets,
    she will want to share with the whole class.

Goldilocks and the Three Bears

retold and illustrated by Jan Brett

retold and illustrated by James Marshall

Summary

These two versions of the traditional tale show how different authors can tell the same story in a variety of ways.

Extension Activities

Class Mural

Read aloud the two versions of *Goldilocks and The Three Bears*. Allow students to examine the pictures in both books. Tell students that they are going to make up their own version of the story. Tape a long piece of butcher paper to the wall and draw at least 12 big squares. Working together, have the class retell the story in the correct sequence. Write the events, one square at a time, using students' actual words. Let them read the sentences back to you. Then assign a square to each student or pair of students. Provide water color markers and have students illustrate their assigned events from the story. Display the mural on the wall in your classroom or in the hallway.

Sample Mural

| Goldilocks went to the woods. | She saw a cottage. | Three bears lived there. |

All About Bears

Read aloud some nonfiction books about bears. Have students pay close attention to details that describe what a real bear's life is like. Place the books in a center so students can examine them.

Real or Fanciful?

Read aloud the storytime version of *Goldilocks and the Three Bears* (pages 34–35). On the chalkboard, draw a two-column chart with the headings *Real* and *Fanciful*. Explain what the words real and fanciful mean. Have students name things or events from the story and determine whether they are real or fanciful.

Extension Activities *(cont.)*

Puppet Play: Marionettes

Have students present "Another Version of Goldilocks and the Three Bears!" (pages 36–39) using marionettes.

Stage: Turn over a long table and cover the surface with white butcher paper. Draw background scenery that shows the inside of the bear's cottage. (See diagram below.) Students should stand behind the table when manipulating their marionette puppets.

Lighting: Obtain two metal workroom bulb frames with clip-on tongs. Put two colored spotlights in them. Clip them onto the back of two chairs and point them toward stage. You may want to plug them into a power strip so that your lines will be grounded. Do not use more than three spotlights per outlet.

Puppets: Make marionette puppets, using three stuffed teddy bears and a blonde doll. Glue two paint sticks together, forming the letter t. Cut four pieces of strong thread into lengths of 30 inches (75 cm) each. Tie the strings onto the ends of the sticks, one string per end. Then tie safety pins to the loose ends of the strings. Fasten the safety pins so the bottoms of the t's connect to the puppets' behinds, the sides connect to the arms, and the tops connect to the heads. Adjust the strings so the ones to the puppets' behinds are the longest, the strings to the arms are shorter, and the ones to the heads are the shortest.

Presentation: Have the class perform the speaking parts, songs, and chants while the puppeteers move the marionette puppets. You may prefer to pretape the script. The script can be done in sections so students can rehearse each part as needed. Then the tape can be played while the puppet show is enacted.

Storytime: *Goldilocks and the Three Bears*

retold by Lynn DiDominicis

Once upon a time there was a little girl named Goldilocks who wanted some excitement in her life. She knew that there was adventure in the woods. One day she decided to go there, even though she knew her mother wouldn't like it. Goldilocks thought she'd be home by suppertime, so off she went!

Meanwhile, in a house deep in the woods, Mama Bear made some porridge for breakfast. The porridge was too hot. So Mama Bear, Papa Bear, and Baby Bear went for their walk before breakfast because they firmly believed in fitness.

When Goldilocks found the bears' cottage, she was delighted! She walked into the kitchen and found the delicious porridge—well, all right, maybe it wasn't delicious, but it was edible. She tried Papa Bear's, and it was too hot! She tried Mama Bear's, and it was too cold! Then she tried Baby Bear's, and it was just right! But she left most of it there anyway because she wasn't all that big on porridge: Goldilocks wandered into the living room to see if the bears had any good videos to watch, and there she saw three chairs. She tried Papa Bear's, and it was too big. She tried Mama Bear's, and it was too soft. Then she tried Baby Bear's, and it seemed all right. Just as she was getting comfortable, the silly chair broke.

Storytime: *Goldilocks and the Three Bears* (cont.)

Well, Goldilocks was getting tired of all this adventure, so she went into the bedroom where she found three beds. She tried Papa Bear's, but it was too hard. She tried Mama Bear's, but it was too soft. Then she tried Baby Bear's. Even though it was a bit small, it felt just right, and she fell fast asleep.

About this time, the three bears finished their walk and came home. They came into the kitchen and saw that someone had sampled their porridge. "Yuck!" said Baby Bear. "Who's been spreading germs in my porridge?"

They went into the living room and Baby Bear cried, "Someone broke my chair! Now can I have a new beanbag chair?"

They all peeked into the bedroom and saw Goldilocks stuffed into Baby Bear's bed, fast asleep. "Get out of my bed before you break it!" cried Baby Bear, scaring poor Goldilocks. She jumped up, but then she saw that she was in the home of three adorable bears. She said she was sorry that she had tasted their porridge and broken the chair. Then she invited Baby Bear to her birthday party. She didn't bother to mention that she needed a bear for one of her party games, "Pin the Belly Button on the Bear."

The End

Another Version of *Goldilocks and The Three Bears!*

by Lynn DiDominicis

Characters:
Goldilocks   Papa Bear   Mama Bear   Baby Bear

Chant: Goldilocks's Song

I want some adventure
And I want it NOW!
I'm tired of waiting
To be allowed.
I know the forest
Is the place to be.
And I'm going to go there
Very merrily!

Goldilocks: I don't want to stay home and take a nap. I'm going to see what's in the forest. I can be home by suppertime. Bye, Mom!

Chant: Oh, no! Don't go!
Don't go into the forest.
You'll have great fear,
(Shouted) You'll disappear!
You won't come out all night!
Oh, no! Don't go!
Don't go into the forest.
You just don't dare,
(Shouted) You'll meet a bear!
You won't come out all night!

Another Version of Goldilocks and The Three Bears! *(cont.)*

(Enter Three Bears into kitchen)
Mama Bear: Now eat the porridge that I made for you, and we will take a nice walk in the forest.

(Chorus says underlined words with actor)
Papa Bear: My porridge is <u>too hot!</u>
Baby Bear: My porridge is <u>too hot!</u>
Mama Bear: My porridge is <u>too hot</u> also. Let's take a walk right now.
(Bears exit)

(Enter Goldilocks into kitchen)
Goldilocks: Oh, look at this darling little house. And someone made some porridge! I can eat some.
(Eats from big bowl)
Goldilocks: Ooo—this porridge is too hot!
(Eats from middle bowl)
Goldilocks: Ooo—this porridge is too cold!
(Eats from small bowl)
Goldilocks: Ooo—this porridge is just right! I'm going to eat it all up.

(Goldilocks goes to living room)
Goldilocks: What a sweet little living room. I think I'll just sit down.
(Sits on big chair)
Goldilocks: Ooo—this chair is too hard.
(Sits on middle chair)
Goldilocks: Ooo—this chair is too soft.
(Sits on baby chair)
Goldilocks: Ooo—this chair is just right. Oh, no! I broke it!

Another Version of Goldilocks and The Three Bears! *(cont.)*

(Goldilocks goes into bedroom)
Goldilocks: Here are the little beds. I am so tired. I think I'll take a short nap.
(Lies on big bed)
Goldilocks: Ooo—This bed is too hard.
(Lies on middle bed)
Goldilocks: Ooo—This bed is too soft.
(Lies on little bed)
Goldilocks: Ooo—This bed is just right.

Song: To the tune of "Lullaby and Good Night"
Lullaby, Goldilocks
Snuggle up in a bed.
You're a long way from home
To the forest you did roam.
But your Mom loves you dear
And she wishes you were near
Go to sleep, Goldilocks
You are safe in a bed.

(Enter Three Bears into kitchen)
Papa Bear: Someone's been eating my porridge!
Mama Bear: Someone's been eating my porridge!
Baby Bear: Someone's been eating my porridge, and now it's all gone!

(Enter Three Bears into living room)
Papa Bear: Someone's been sitting in my chair.
Mama Bear: Someone's been sitting in my chair.
Baby Bear: Someone's been sitting in my chair, and now it's broken!

Another Version of Goldilocks and The Three Bears! *(cont.)*

(Enter Three Bears into bedroom)

Papa Bear: Someone's been sleeping in my bed.

Mama Bear: Someone's been sleeping in my bed.

Baby Bear: Someone's been sleeping in my bed, and there she is now!

Goldilocks: *(waking up)* Oh, my goodness! You are such cute little bears. I am sorry that I ate your porridge, broke your chair, and slept in your little bed. I just wanted to see what was in the forest.

Mama Bear: There, there. It's all right. But you must go home now because your mommy will be worried about you.

Papa Bear: Yes, I'll take you to the edge of the forest so that you won't get lost.

Baby Bear: Can I go? Please, can I go, too? Please?

Papa Bear: Okay, you can come along.

Chant: Good-bye To The Bears

We had some adventure
In the forest today.
We made some new friends
Along the way.

Goldilocks: I'm going back there
My new friends to see!
We know the forest
Is the place to be
And we'll all go back there
Very merrily!

"Jack and the Beanstalk" from *Fairy Tales*

retold by James Riordan

Summary

Jack sells the family cow for some magic beans that grow into a giant beanstalk. He gets more than he bargains for when he climbs the beanstalk and encounters a giant. His adventures end happily when he escapes back down the beanstalk.

Extension Activities

Grow "Magic" Beans

Have students grow some "magic" beans using the following directions.

Materials:

- one reclosable plastic bag per student
- three or four cotton balls per student, soaked in water
- seeds (Regular lima beans or other dry beans from the supermarket work well. Soak them overnight before using.)

Directions: Place the bean seeds in the reclosable plastic bags with several wet cotton balls. The seeds will "magically" sprout in several days. You may wish to show students how to use a ruler to measure the growth of the seeds. Record the measurements on a class graph. Then, send the seeds home to be planted in the ground.

Oral Language Organizer: Story Map

Reproduce the story map (page 41) on a large piece of butcher paper or the chalkboard. Read aloud the traditional version of *Jack and the Beanstalk* (pages 42–43). Work with students to complete the story map using this version of the story.

Reproduce the story map (page 41) on a large piece of butcher paper or the chalkboard. Read aloud the play "Jack and the Spaceship Beanstalk" (pages 51–56). Then work together to complete the story map using this version of the story.

You may also wish to have students complete a third story map that shows similarities and differences between the two versions of the story.

Presenting a Play

Have students present the play, "Jack and the Spaceship Beanstalk" (pages 51–56). Patterns for simple costumes are provided (pages 46–50). Staging ideas are also suggested (pages 44–45).

Story Map

New Vocabulary Words: (The whole class should brainstorm a list and define the words.)	Title: Author: (Ask volunteers to draw pictures.)	Setting: (Where and when)
	Character: (Describe) Character: (Describe)	Character: (Describe) Character: (Describe)
	Plot: (Sequence of Events)	Problem/Conflict:
	Problem Resolution:	Personal Reaction: (Each student writes a sentence.)

Storytime: *Jack and the Beanstalk*

retold by Lynn DiDominicis

Once upon a time, there was a young boy named Jack who lived with his mother. They were very poor. One day, Jack's mother asked him to take their only cow to town and sell it so they could buy some food.

Jack started for town with the cow, but on the way he met a man who was selling magic beans. The man told Jack that he would trade a bag of magic beans for the cow. Now Jack was a very smart boy, and he realized that the beans were worth much more than the cow. So he made the trade. When he got home, he showed the beans to his mother. Jack's mother did not understand how valuable the magic beans were, and she was very upset. She sent Jack to his room without supper, which was all right because they didn't have any supper anyway.

Jack decided his mother knew something he didn't, so he threw the beans out the window and went to bed. When he woke up the next morning, he noticed right away that the sun was not shining in his room. He looked out the window, and there was the BIGGEST beanstalk he had ever seen. Jack did what any young boy would do—he began to climb it.

When he got to the top, among the clouds, he saw a castle off in the distance. He knew what that meant! Food! So he ran to the castle. He barely made it inside as the moat bridge was being lifted. He sniffed and followed his nose to the kitchen. The furniture was very large. When he got to the kitchen, he saw why. This was the home of a giant.

"Fee, fi, fo, fum, I smell the blood of an Englishman!" said the giant. Jack thought this was an odd way of greeting a guest, but he said hello anyway. The giant said, "I'm going to eat you for breakfast!" Jack thought such a fine castle must have better food than him, so he decided to distract the giant while he looked. He offered to play a song on the giant's magic harp. Of course, because it was a magic harp, the giant went right to sleep, even though he had just woken up. Then, Jack saw a magic hen, and visions of scrambled eggs danced in his head. Unfortunately, the hen only laid golden eggs, so he gathered up the magic harp and the magic hen and ran for the beanstalk.

42

Storytime: *Jack and the Beanstalk* (cont.)

Meanwhile, Jack's mother woke up and went out in the yard, just to see if the cow was really gone. Immediately, she noticed the beanstalk. These things are hard to miss. She called her neighbor, the woodsman, to come over right away with his hatchet. "Cut this thing down," she said. "What will the neighbors think?" So the woodsman began to chop with his hatchet. All of a sudden, they spied Jack on his way down with something in his arms. Now Jack's mother wasn't in the mood for any more foolishness, so she told the woodsman to keep chopping. Just as he made the last CHOP, Jack dropped into the yard. He showed his mother the magic harp and the magic hen, and like any good mother, she realized that their problems were over. They killed the hen and had fried chicken for supper. The golden eggs made a lovely centerpiece, and the magic harp played wonderful music.

Creative Drama Instructions

Props

Make the props described below and on page 45 before presenting *Jack and the Spaceship Beanstalk* (pages 51–56).

Spaceship

Make a cardboard cutout of a spaceship as shown in the diagram below. Spray paint and decorate the ship. Cut a hole in the center at the bottom of the ship. Stand up the spaceship, using cardboard strips and gluing them on as shown. The side strips can be reinforced with wooden slats. Multi-colored Christmas lights can be added for effect. Tape a "whooshing" sound effect by blowing through a paper towel roll. Put talcum powder in the bottom of another paper towel roll and lay it on its side. Blow the talcum powder through the paper towel roll and out the hole at the bottom of the spaceship during "take off." Be sure the powder is not inhaled.

Robot

Make a robot out of a large cardboard box and several shoe boxes. Wire spring toys or compressible tubing can be used for the arms. Use the diagram shown below as a guide.

Box

Decorate a large cardboard box as shown below.

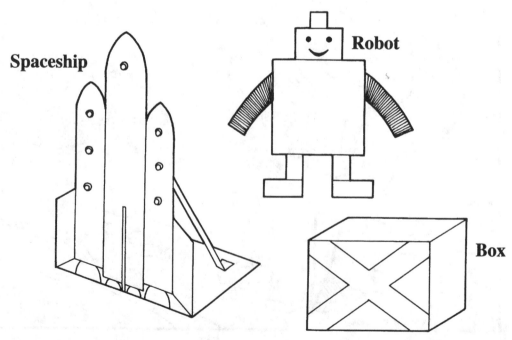

Spaceship

Robot

Box

Creative
Drama Instructions *(cont.)*

Rock

Create a large rock by making big balls out of newspaper. Put the balls together and wind masking tape around them until they look like one giant ball. Then spray paint it gray so it looks like a rock.

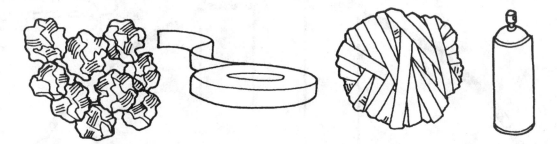

Background

Draw the background on butcher paper and tape it onto a wall. For an interesting effect, use twinkling white Christmas lights for the stars.

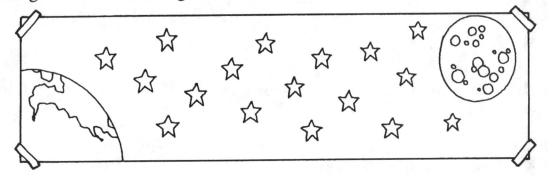

Lighting

Make a "spotlight" using a yellow transparency and black paper. Cut a hole in the middle of the black paper and place it over the yellow transparency. Use it on an overhead projector.

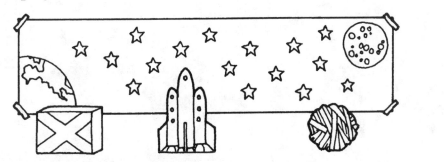

Headband Hat Patterns

Jack

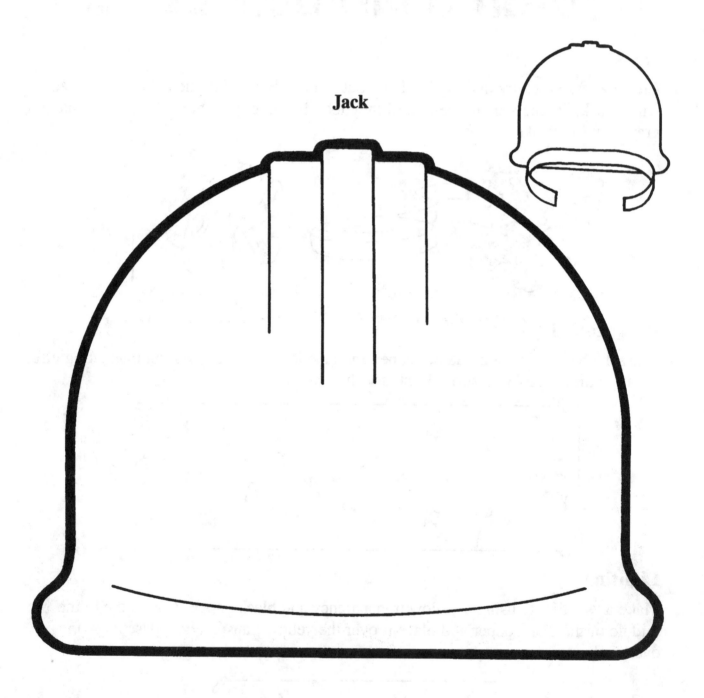

Headband Hat Patterns *(cont.)*

Space Captain

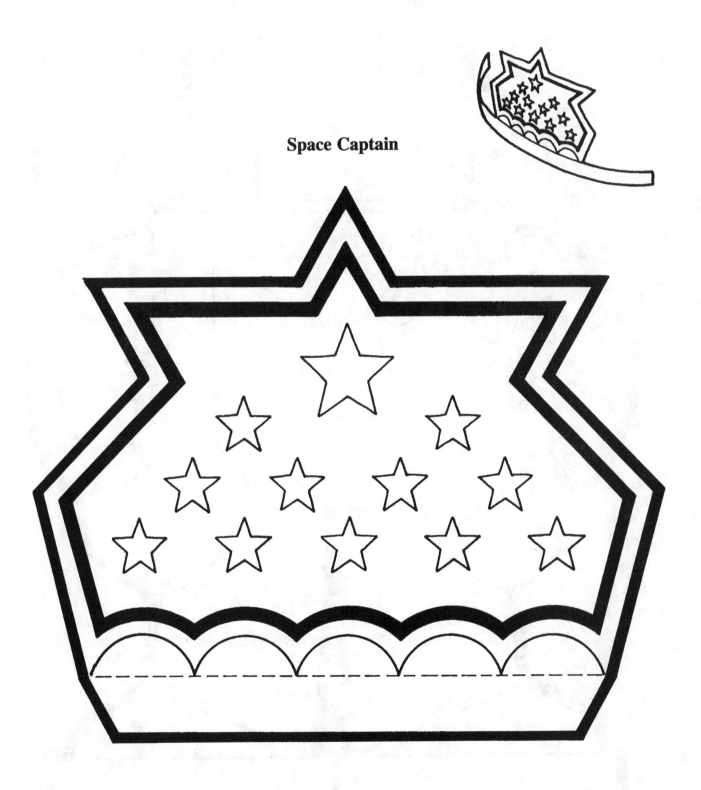

Headband Hat Patterns (cont.)

Android Giant

48

Headband Hat Patterns (cont.)

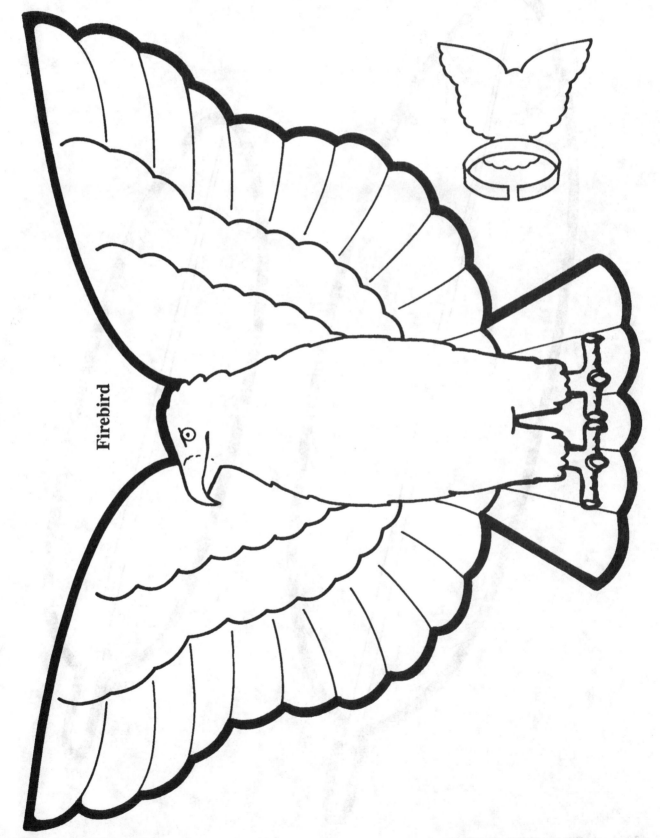

Firebird

Firebird Tail Feathers

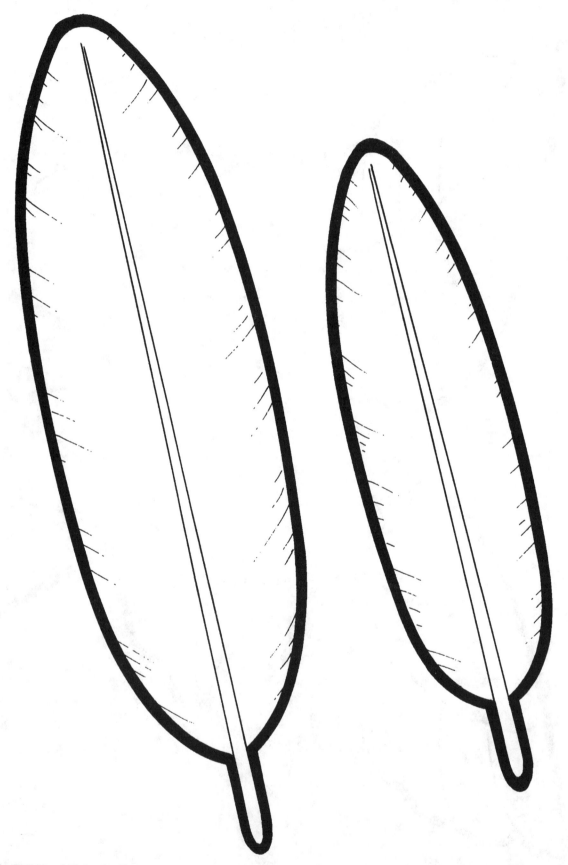

Jack and the Spaceship Beanstalk

by Lynn DiDominicis

Characters:	
Space Captain	Android Giant
Jack	Firebird

(Space Captain enters, center stage)

Space Captain: Jack! Come in here! Now where is that boy? He's never around when I need him!

Jack: Coming, Captain, sir!

(Jack enters)

Space Captain: Jack, we have a problem. Our robot's battery is dead. Take him over to the next galaxy and get him repaired.

Jack: Okay, don't worry. I'll take care of everything.

(Jack exits with robot)

Space Captain: I hope I haven't made a big mistake. I never know what that boy will do.

(Exits)

(Enter Jack with a small box)

Jack: Captain, oh, Captain, sir! He's going to be so proud of me when he sees what I've done.

(Enter Space Captain)

Jack and the Spaceship Beanstalk *(cont.)*

Jack: Oh, there you are, sir.

Space Captain: Did you get the robot repaired?

Jack: Well, yes and no.

Space Captain: What do you mean, yes and no?

Jack: Well, I brought the robot into the shop but they didn't have the battery it needs. I started to go to the next shop...

Space Captain: Good boy. Shows you're thinking.

Jack: . . . when the clerk said he would be getting some new batteries tomorrow and could fix the robot then. He told me to leave it and he'd call me when it was ready.

Space Captain: So you left it?

Jack: Well, yes and no.

Space Captain: What do you mean yes and no?

Jack: Well, I started to leave. Just then the little robot got a power surge and started flying off down the street. I chased right after it, sir.

Space Captain: Did you catch it?

Jack: Well, yes and no.

 Space Captain: What do you mean, yes and no?

Jack and the Spaceship Beanstalk *(cont.)*

Jack: Well, I caught it but I bumped into this Android Giant. He said, "What a fine looking robot! How much will you sell it for?" I told him that it was broken.

Space Captain: So you didn't sell the robot?

Jack: Well, yes I did. The Android Giant said he'd take it, broken and all, for this box and the magic that's inside it.

Space Captain: And you fell for that?

Jack: Yes, sir. This is a magic box!

Space Captain: Oh, no! A ten million dollar robot for a magic box! Where did I go wrong?

(Space Captain exits)

(Jack sits on the floor and opens box. Takes out a piece of paper.)

Jack: Hmmm. Here are some instructions. It says, "Sprinkle magic dust on spaceship. Get into spaceship."

(Jack goes to spaceship, sprinkles dust, and enters. Spaceship takes off.)

Spaceship TAKE-OFF:
Lights flash on and off. Play tape of "whooshing" sound effect made by blowing through a paper towel roll. Blow talcum powder through paper towel roll, out hole in bottom of spaceship.
(Jack exits spaceship)

Jack: Wow! Where am I?

Jack and the Spaceship

(Android Giant enters from opposite side)

Android Giant: Fee, fie, fo, fan, I smell the blood of a spaceship man.

Jack: Oh, no, Mr. Android Giant, sir. I'm just a little boy.

Android Giant: Well, come along with me, and I'll decide what to do with you.

(Both exit)

(Enter Space Captain)

Space Captain: Jack, where are you?

(Sees box, picks it up, and reads instructions)

Space Captain: Oh, no! I have to find him!

(Sprinkles spaceship with dust, enters ship, and ship takes off.)

(Space Captain exits ship.)

Space Captain: Jack . . . Jack. Where are you?

(Space Captain exits)

(Android Giant and Jack enter from other side. Android Giant sits on a rock.)

Android Giant: Okay, Jack, sing for me. Dance for me.

Jack: Would you like to hear a lullaby?

Android Giant: Oh, yes.

Jack and the Spaceship
Beanstalk *(cont.)*

Jack: (sings to the tune "Rock-a-bye Baby")
Rock-a-bye giant
On the space rock
When the moon beams
The space rock will drop.
(To himself) What a dumb song. Shhh! He's going to sleep.

(Enter Space Captain)

Space Captain: Jack! I didn't think I'd ever find you. Who's he?

Jack: He's an Android Giant, and I think he wants to keep me.

Space Captain: Sprinkle some dust on the spaceship, and let's get out of here!

Jack: What do you mean, magic dust? I don't have any left! You sprinkle some dust on there.

Space Captain: Me? Why is it always up to me? I don't have any dust left!

Jack and Space Captain: Uh-Oh!

Space Captain: Look, maybe there's enough magic dust left on the spaceship. Let's get in and see what happens.

(Both enter spaceship—nothing happens. Both exit)

Space Captain: Great! Now what are we going to do?

Jack: *(Crying)* I don't know. You're supposed to know what to do.

Jack and the Spaceship Beanstalk (cont.)

(Enter Firebird)

Firebird: Tweet! Tweet! What's the trouble here?

Jack: *(Crying)* We sprinkled magic dust on this spaceship, and it brought us here. Now this giant wants to keep us. We want to go home, but we're out of magic dust.

Firebird: Oh, you poor thing. But that's no problem. That Android Giant is magic. He has to have some magic dust on him somewhere.

(Firebird starts to poke and prod. Android Giant stirs.)

Jack: Oh, no! Leave him alone! You'll wake him up!

Space Captain: I have an idea. But I need one of your tail feathers.

Firebird: What? In your dreams, buddy! No way!

(Firebird jumps in circles. Space Captain grabs and pulls a feather from his tail.)

Firebird: Ouch! That hurt!

Space Captain: Okay, everyone. Stand back! Here goes!

(Space Captain tickles Android Giant's nose. Android Giant sneezes.)

Space Captain: Quick, everyone into the spaceship!

(Space Captain, Jack, and Firebird cram into spaceship. Firebird gets pushed back out. Ship takes off.)

Firebird: Well! That's appreciation for you. Oh, well—I

The Three Little Pigs

by Teacher Created Materials

Summary

Three little pigs build houses out of straw, sticks and bricks. The wolf blows down the houses built of straw and sticks, but the pigs are safe in the house built of bricks.

Extension Activities

Character Patterns

Have students use the character patterns (page 58) to retell the story.

Making Little Books

Have students make little books (pages 59–62). Read the story together. Encourage students to take home their little books to share with family members. You may wish to read aloud other stories about pigs. See the bibliography (pages 143 and 144).

Oral Language Organizer: Pocket Chart Patterns

Use the sentence strips and a pocket chart (page 63) to discover patterns and rhymes in this story.

Example 1: May I have some **straw** to build a house?

May I have some **sticks** to build a house?

May I have some **bricks** to build a house?

*Call students' attention to repeated patterns. Ask which words are the same and which change.

*Visually match each line, word, sound.

Example 2: When the wolf came by and said, "Let me **in**!" "Not by the hair of my chinny chin **chin**!"

*Match the words that sound alike.

*Discuss sequence. Take out major phrases and have students put them back where they belong.

Example 3: So the wolf **huffed** and he **puffed**

*Take away words that do not match.

Rap

A rap tells a story using matching rhythms and rhyming words. It emphasizes words and patterns by repeating them. The leader should read the rap and have the students repeat the italicized words. Establish a rhythm pattern by snapping.

Building Blocks

Allow students to examine some straw, sticks and bricks. Help students make comparative statements, such as "A brick is heavier than a stick."

Character Patterns

Directions: Color and cut out the Three Little Pigs and the Wolf. Use these pictures for retelling the story.

Making Little Books

My Little Book of The Three Little Pigs Rap

Name _____

One pig built his house of straw.
Oh, no! Oh, no!

1

Making Little Books (cont.)

One pig built his house of sticks.
Oh, no! Oh, no!

2

One pig built his house of bricks.
Smart pig! Smart pig!

3

Making Little Books (cont.)

**Then the wolf came to blow them down.
Huff, puff! Huff, puff!**

4

**Down went the house of straw and sticks.
Huff, puff! Huff, puff!**

5

Making Little Books (cont.)

But he couldn't blow down the house of bricks.

Huff, puff! Huff, puff!

6

Who's afraid of the big bad wolf?

Not us! Not us!

7

Pocket Chart

Directions:

Make sentence strips using the examples below. Cut out rectangles from colored transparencies that match the length of the emphasized words and the width of the sentence strips. Place them over the words rather than removing them. The words will show through three or four layers of transparencies.

Sentence Strips:

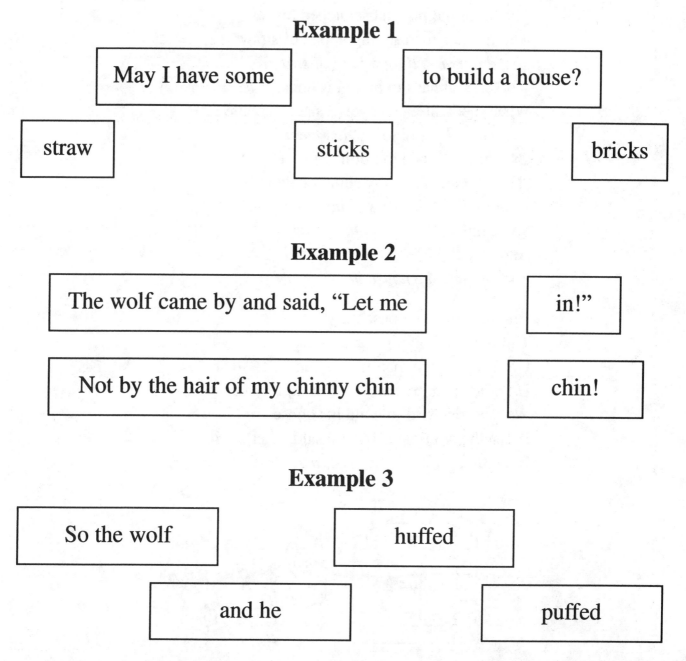

Example 1

May I have some		to build a house?
straw	sticks	bricks

Example 2

The wolf came by and said, "Let me   in!"

Not by the hair of my chinny chin   chin!

Example 3

So the wolf   huffed

and he   puffed

Three Little Pigs Rap

by Lynn DiDominicis

Once upon a time in a land far away
There were three little pigs   *three little pigs*
They went to seek their fortune and soon they found
They had to find a way to build a house.
Had to find a way to build a house.

The first little pig just scratched his jaw
And found a man selling a load of straw
Found a man selling a load of straw
Worked real hard to build his house
When the wolf came by and said, "Let me in!"
Wolf came by and said, "Let me in!"
"No, no, no," said the little pig,
"Not by the hair of my chinny chin chin."
"Not by the hair of my chinny chin chin."
So he huffed   *so he huffed*
And he puffed   *and he puffed*
And he blew the house in.

And he blew the house in.
The second little pig was in a fix
Until he found a man with a bundle of sticks
Until he found a man with a bundle of sticks
Worked real hard to build his house
When the wolf came by and said, "Let me in!"
Wolf came by and said, "Let me in!"

Three Little Pigs Rap *(cont.)*

"No, no, no," said the little pig,
"Not by the hair of my chinny chin chin."
"Not by the hair of my chinny chin chin."
So he huffed   *So he huffed*
And he puffed   *And he puffed*
And he blew the house in.
And he blew the house in.

The third little pig was out of tricks
When he met a man selling a pile of bricks
Met a man selling a pile of bricks
Worked real hard to build his house
When the wolf came by and said, "Let me in!"
Wolf came by and said, "Let me in!"
"No, no, no," said the little pig,
"Not by the hair on my chinny chin chin."
"Not by the hair on my chinny chin chin."
So he huffed   *So he huffed*
And he puffed   *And he puffed*
And he couldn't blow the house in.
Couldn't blow the house in.

Into the chimney   *Into the chimney*
Wolf went in a flash   *Wolf went in a flash*
Ended his life   *Ended his life*
With a thud and a splash   *With a thud and a splash*

The moral of the story is clear to see
The moral of the story is clear to see
Build your house of bricks, you'll never have to flee.
Build your house of bricks, you'll never have to flee.
Oh, yeah Oh, yeah
Oh, yeah Oh, yeah
Oh, yeah Oh, yeah

"The Three Billy Goats Gruff"

by Tomie dePaola

Summary

Some favorite traditional nursery tale is from Tomie dePaola's Faorite Nursery Tales *are retold with new illustrations.*

Extension Activities

Using Flannel Board Pieces

A "Billy Goats Gruff" flannel board set can be purchased from any teacher resource store or from a teacher resource catalog.

Create your own flannel board. Use a piece of flannel for the background. Cut out the patterns (pages 67–69), color them, and put Velcro circles on the backs. The Velcro can be purchased at an office supply store. A pattern for a background scene is provided (page 79). You may wish to add trees, flowers, and a hillside.

To make the reading of the story easier, tape record the story first. Then you can manipulate the figures on the flannel board without juggling the book.

Sequencing Activity

Have the students tell the events of the story in order by manipulating the flannel board pieces. You may also wish to have students use the flannel board pieces as you read the storytime version (pages 70 and 71).

Hear It/See It

Put the words "Trip Trap Trip Trap"on the flannel board using the pattern provided. Reread the story. Have the students say "Trip Trap Trip Trap" at the appropriate times and have a student point to the words.

Trip Trap Trip Trap

Making Little Books

Have students make little books of *The Three Billy Goats Gruff* (pages 72–75). Encourage them to share the books with family members.

The Troll's Story

Have students use life-size puppets to retell the story from the troll's point of view (pages 76–81).

Lace Cards

Have students improve fine motor skills by using the goat and troll lace cards (page 82).

Flannel Board Patterns

big

youngest

middle

Flannel Board Patterns *(cont.)*

troll

Flannel Board Patterns (cont.)

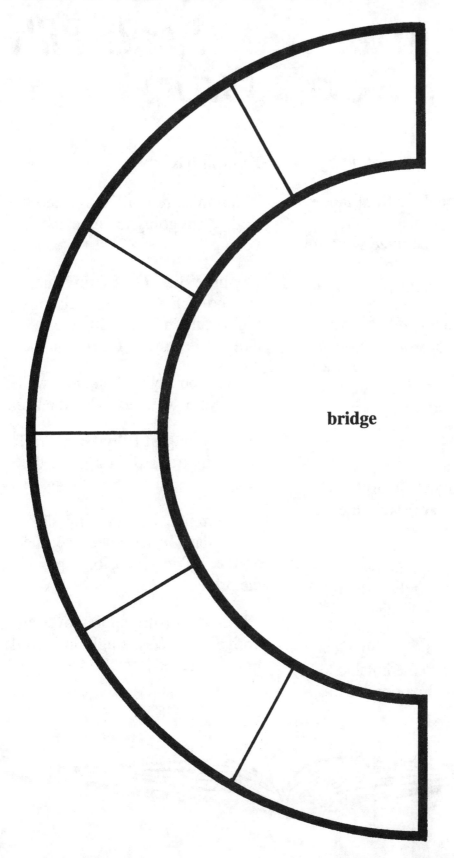

bridge

Storytime: *The Three Billy Goats Gruff*

retold by Lynn DiDominicis

Once upon a time there lived three billy goats, and the name of all three was Gruff. The three wanted to go up to the hillside to eat grass to make themselves fat.

In order to get to the hillside they had to cross over a wooden bridge that was over a stream. Under the bridge lived an ugly little troll with enormous eyes and a very, very long nose.

The first to reach the bridge was the youngest Billy Goat Gruff. "Trip, trap, trip, trap!" went the bridge.

"Who's that trip trapping over my bridge?" roared the ugly little troll from underneath the bridge.

"It's only me, tiny little Billy Goat Gruff. I'm going to the hillside to eat grass," he said in a tiny little voice.

"Oh no you're not!" thundered the troll. "I'm going to come and eat you up."

The little Billy Goat Gruff said, "Oh no, don't eat me. Wait for my brother, the middle Billy Goat Gruff. He's much fatter than me."

"Fatter you say? Then, very well, be on your way," growled the troll.

So the youngest Billy Goat Gruff went trip, trap, trip, trap over the bridge.

A few minutes later the middle Billy Goat Gruff started over the bridge. "Trip, trap trip, trap!" went the bridge.

"Who's that trip trapping over my bridge?" roared the ugly little troll from underneath the bridge.

Storytime: *The Three Billy Goats Gruff* (cont.)

"It's only me, medium-sized Billy Goat Gruff. I'm going to the hillside to eat grass," he said in medium-sized voice.

"Oh no you're not!" thundered the troll. "I'm going to come and eat you up."

The middle Billy Goat Gruff said, "Oh no, don't eat me. Wait for my brother, the big Billy Goat Gruff. He's much fatter than me."

"Fatter, you say? Then, very well, be on your way," growled the troll.

So the middle Billy Goat Gruff went trip, trap, trip, trap over the bridge.

Soon the big Billy Goat Gruff appeared. "Trip, trap, trip, trap!" went the bridge.

"Who's that trip trapping over my bridge?" roared the ugly little troll from underneath the bridge.

"It's only me, big Billy Goat Gruff. I'm going to the hillside to eat grass," he said in a great big voice.

"Oh no you're not!" thundered the troll, "I'm going to come and eat you up."

"Come up and try to eat me!" shouted the big Billy Goat Gruff.

The ugly little troll climbed to the top of the bridge. Then the big Billy Goat Gruff flew at the troll with his sharp horns, causing him to turn somersaults off the bridge and into the stream. The troll was never seen again.

Big Billy Goat Gruff went trip, trap, trip, trap over the bridge to eat grass on the hillside with his brothers. And there the three Billy Goats Gruff can still be found, as long as there's grass on the hill!

Making Little Books

My Little Book of The Three Billy Goats

Name _____

**The three goats are hungry
For something to eat.
Trip, trap, trip, trap.**

1

Making Little Books (cont.)

**But under the bridge
Watch out for the troll!
Trip, trap, trip, trap.**

2

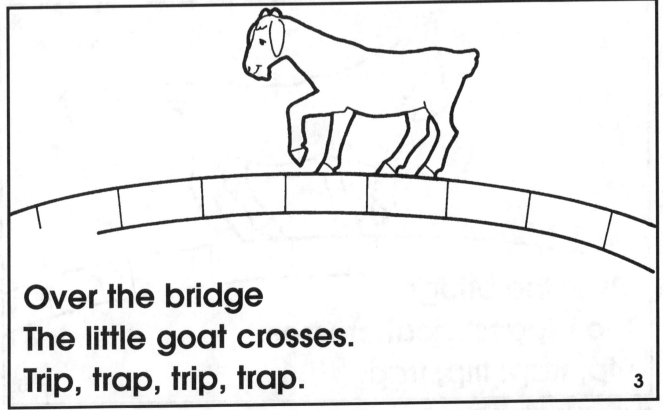

**Over the bridge
The little goat crosses.
Trip, trap, trip, trap.**

3

Making Little Books (cont.)

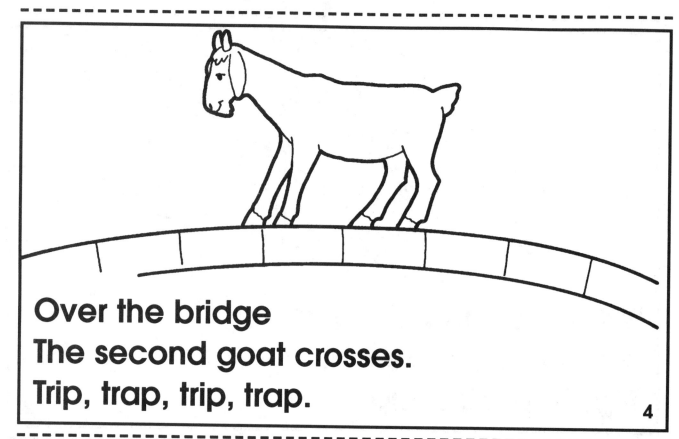

**Over the bridge
The second goat crosses.
Trip, trap, trip, trap.**

4

**Over the bridge
The biggest goat crosses.
Trip, trap, trip, trap.**

5

Making Little Books (cont.)

Off the bridge goes the troll
And the goats have their lunch.
Trip, trap, trip, trap.

6

The three goats' story
Has come to an end.
Snip, snap, snout,
This tale's told out.

7

Creative Drama Instructions

The Story: Instead of presenting the traditional story of the three billy goats, tell the story from the troll's point of view. Have a class discussion about how the troll might have felt and what he could have done to get along better with the billy goats.

Characters: Using the patterns provided (pages 77 and 78), make life-sized cardboard puppets for the actors to carry. These puppets can be created by making a transparency from the patterns, shining the images up on the wall, and tracing the outlines onto butcher paper that is taped there. If you prefer, you can draw them onto the butcher paper freehand, using the patterns as models. After the patterns are drawn, cut holes for the faces. Laminate them to minimize damage. Then, glue them onto pieces of cardboard. Recut the holes for the faces.

Staging: Background scenery can be created by using an overhead projector and a transparency. Make a plain transparency of the pattern provided (page 79). Color the transparency with watercolor markers. Put the transparency on an overhead projector. Place the overhead projector on the floor. Shine the transparency onto the wall at an angle so that the actors do not interfere with the image. See diagram below.

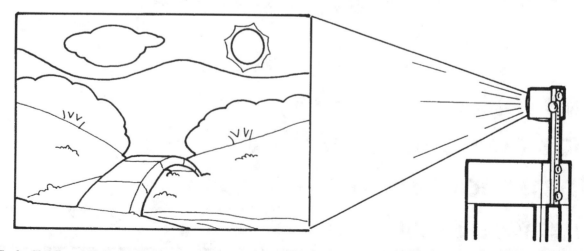

Life-size Puppet Patterns

Directions: Draw this pattern, freehand or from a transparency of this page, to make all three billy goats. Adjust for the different sizes of the billy goats.

Billy Goat Pattern

Life-size Puppet Patterns *(cont.)*

Directions: Draw this pattern, freehand or from a transparency of this page, to make the troll.

Troll Pattern

Background Transparency Pattern

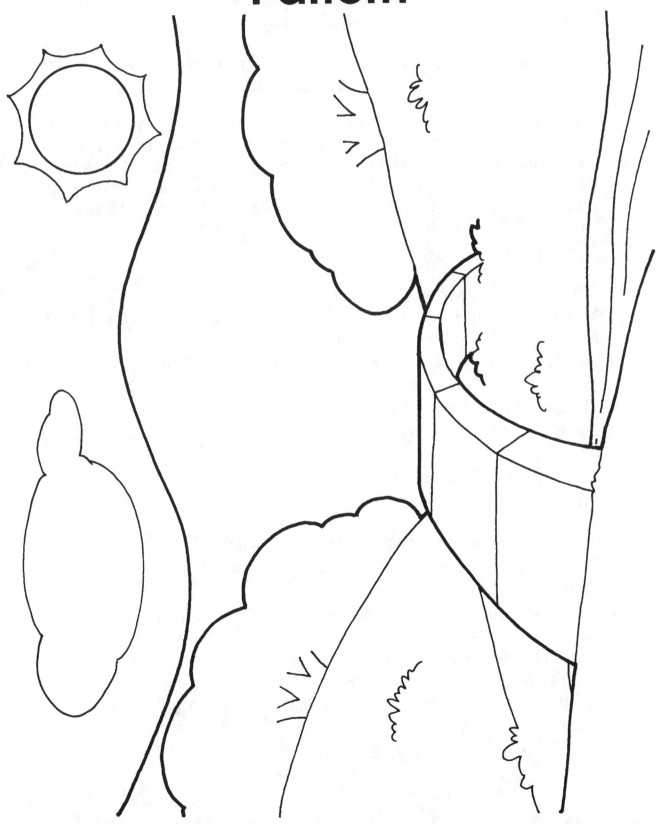

The Troll's Story

by Lynn DiDominicis

Characters:

Troll   Small Billy Goat   Middle Billy Goat   Big Billy Goat

---

Troll: *(To audience)* Oh, hello there. Allow me to introduce myself. I am the Troll. I wanted to talk to you for a moment before those three pesky billy goats get here to torment me again this morning. You see, I am a very nice, quiet, well-mannered troll. But those billy goats are about to drive me crazy! Uh oh, here they come. Now you'll see what I mean. I'd better hide!

(Crouches under bridge.)

(Enter Three Billy Goats, stage front)

Small Billy Goat: I don't see the troll yet. What shall we do to him today?

Middle Billy Goat: Let's tackle him and pull his whiskers!

Big Billy Goat: No, we did that last week. Let's take off his boots and throw them into the stream!

Middle Billy Goat: Phew! Bad idea!

Small Billy Goat: Well, we can always sneak up behind him and yell, "Boo!" That always gets him.

Big Billy Goat: That's right. Okay, let's go.

(Exit, stage left)

(Troll moves to stage right, other side of the bridge)

Small Billy Goat: *(Enters from stage left)* Trip, trap, trip, trap.

Troll: Who is crossing my bridge?

Small Billy Goat: It is I, the littlest Billy Goat Gruff. I want to eat grass on the other side of the bridge.

Troll: *(Meekly)* Well, this is my bridge and if you cross, I'll just eat you up—*(Aside)* just kidding, of course.

Small Billy Goat: Why don't you wait for my brother. He's even bigger. There's more to eat, you know.

Troll: Well, I suppose I could do that.

The Troll's Story *(cont.)*

Small Billy Goat: Good. Now move. Boo!

Troll: *(Jumps and crouches under bridge)* I just hate it when they do that!

(Small Billy Goat crosses)

(Troll comes out again)

Middle Billy Goat: *(Enters from stage left)* Trip, trap, trip, trap.

Troll: Who is crossing my bridge?

Middle Billy Goat: It is I, the middle Billy Goat Gruff, and I want to eat grass on the other side of the bridge.

Troll: Your little brother was just here and he said that I could eat you up. But I would never do that to such a nice billy goat as you.

Middle Billy Goat: Good! Wait for my big brother. He'll be even more for you to eat. Now move! Boo!

Troll: *(Jumps and crouches again)* He did it, too! It must run in the family!

(Middle Billy Goat crosses over)

(Troll comes out again)

Big Billy Goat: *(Enters from stage left)* Trip, trap, trip, trap.

Troll: Who is crossing my bridge?

Big Billy Goat: It is I, big Billy Goat Gruff, and I want to eat grass on the other side of the bridge.

Troll: Your brothers were already here, and they said you would take me out to dinner.

Big Billy Goat: You mean you don't want to eat me up?

Troll: Of course not! I don't even like goat. I like hamburgers!

Big Billy Goat: Well, why didn't you say so? C'mon! Let's go get burgers and fries!

(Walk off arm in arm)

Lace Cards

troll

goat

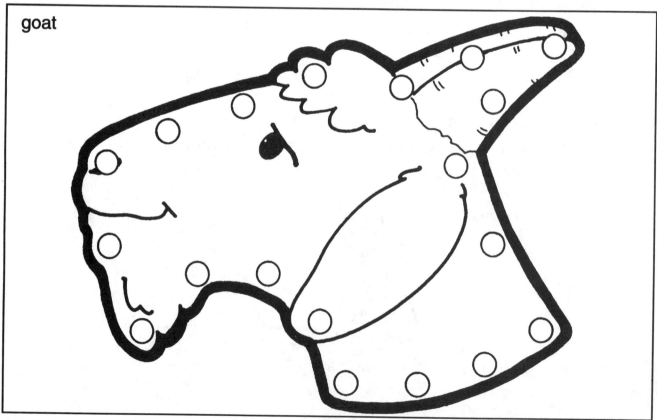

82

Tomie dePaola's Mother Goose

by Tomie dePaola

Summary

Tomie dePaola takes common nursery rhymes and retells them, adding new illustrations.

Extension Activities

Rhyming Words

Work with students to identify rhyming words (page 84). Then, have a volunteer give a word and ask students to name other words that rhyme. Continue with other volunteers.

Clerihews

The clerihew is a brief, humorous four-line poem about a person or character. It is named after Edmund Clerihew Bentley (1875-1956), an English writer of detective stories who invented this form of verse. Help students write some clerihews based on stories from Tomie dePaola's book.

Clerihew Structure:
Line 1: Ends with the person's name
Line 2: Rhymes with line 1
Lines 3 & 4: Rhyme with each other

Examples:

Yankee Doodle's horse named Bob,
Likes to eat corn on the cob.
Eating corn is not much fun,
But he says it helps him run.

Poor and sickly Jack and Jill,
Doctor made them take a pill.
They won't cry, and they don't care,
They'll pour honey in their hair.

by Lynn DiDominicis

TV Tidbits

Have students present their clerihews as part of a TV comedy show (page 85). You may wish to present the comedy show to other classes, parents, or at a PTA meeting.

Rhyming Activity

Directions: In each box, circle the picture below that rhymes with the top picture.

Creative Drama Instructions

TV Tidbits

Obtain a large, cardboard appliance box. Cut out a square from the front. Paint and decorate it to look like a television. See the diagram below. Cut a flap in the back for entering and exiting.

Have students compose original clerihews. With very young students, you may need to help them and then have them memorize their clerihews.

Perform the clerihews on a TV program entitled "The Clerihew Comedy Hour." You may even want to get into the TV box yourself and act as the master of ceremonies, introducing each act.

These clerihews can also be sung to the tune of "Mary Had a Little Lamb" by adding extra notes here and there. This will help younger students learn the verses more quickly.

Tell students to remember the following things when they present their clerihews:

- Stand up straight.
- Face the audience.
- Speak clearly and loudly.

Swimmy

by Leo Lionni

Summary

Swimmy was the only black fish among many red fish. When a big, fierce tuna ate the red fish, he had to learn to protect himself in the beautiful ocean.

Extension Activities

Alphabet Aquarium

Did you know that you can fill an aquarium with fish whose names begin with each letter of the alphabet? If an aquarium is available to you, ask your local pet store to help you fill it with these fish. Invite parents to get involved. If you cannot obtain the actual fish, draw pictures of the different types on a classroom mural.

Puppet Show: Swimmy

Stage: Use a cardboard pattern-cutting board that folds. This can be purchased at any fabric store. Spray paint the outside and decorate it so that it looks like underwater plant life and fish.

Lighting: Work lights with metal shields and grips for fastening to chairs make an interesting lighting effect. These can be purchased at hardware stores. Use colored light bulbs in them. If you use more than one, plug them into a multi-plug power strip.

Music: Obtain a tape of Raffi singing "Baby Beluga."

Special Effects: You will need a bottle of bubbles and a wand from the grocery store. You will also need a straw and a large bowl of water.

Puppets: Have students cut out the stick puppets from the patterns provided (pages 88-94). Have them color the puppets the appropriate colors according to the story. You may wish to laminate the puppets to minimize wear. Glue the puppets to craft sticks.

Fish Kite

Have students make a fish kite (page 95) and tell stories about how their fish are special.

Origami Fish

Have students improve fine motor skills by folding a paper square into the shape of a fish (page 96).

Puppet Show

Script: The script is the actual story, *Swimmy.* Follow the instructions to put on the show. It is suggested that you record the dialogue and sound effects. Then play the tape while the puppeteers perform.

Instructions

Opening: Swimmy is on stage by himself and sings to the song, "Baby Beluga." One student sits behind this puppeteer, located behind the stage, and blows bubbles from the bubble bottle into the air. This will create the illusion of being underwater.

Story: Puppeteers act out the story as it is being read. An occasional background bubbling sound effect can be done by blowing hard through a straw into a big bowl of water.

Ending: All of the characters are on stage and sing the song, "Baby Beluga." Again, the bubble blower blows bubbles from behind.

Use this space to plan your performance:

1. Who will design the background?

2. Who will be the puppeteers?

3. Who will do the special effects?

4. Who will run the tape recorded story?

Stick Puppet Patterns

Sea Scene

Black Fish

Stick Puppet Patterns *(cont.)*

Swimmy and Friends

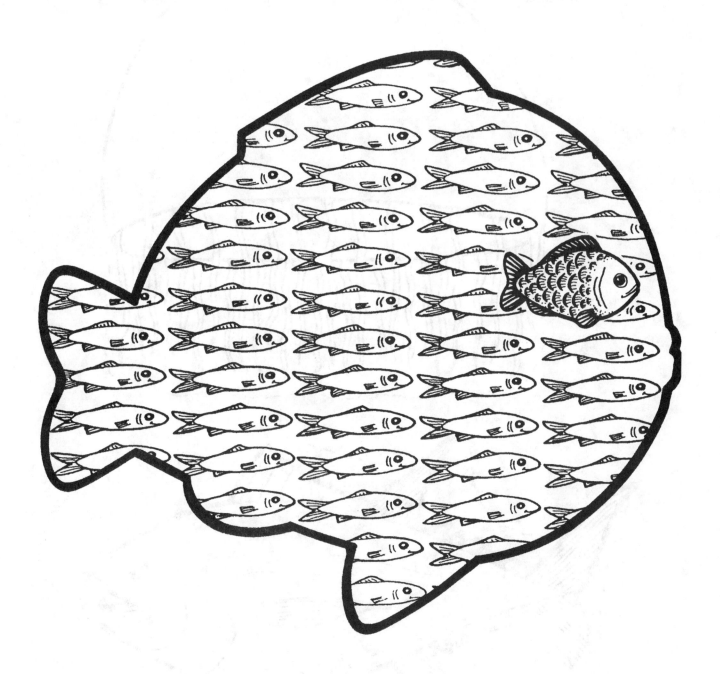

Stick Puppet Patterns *(cont.)*

Medusa

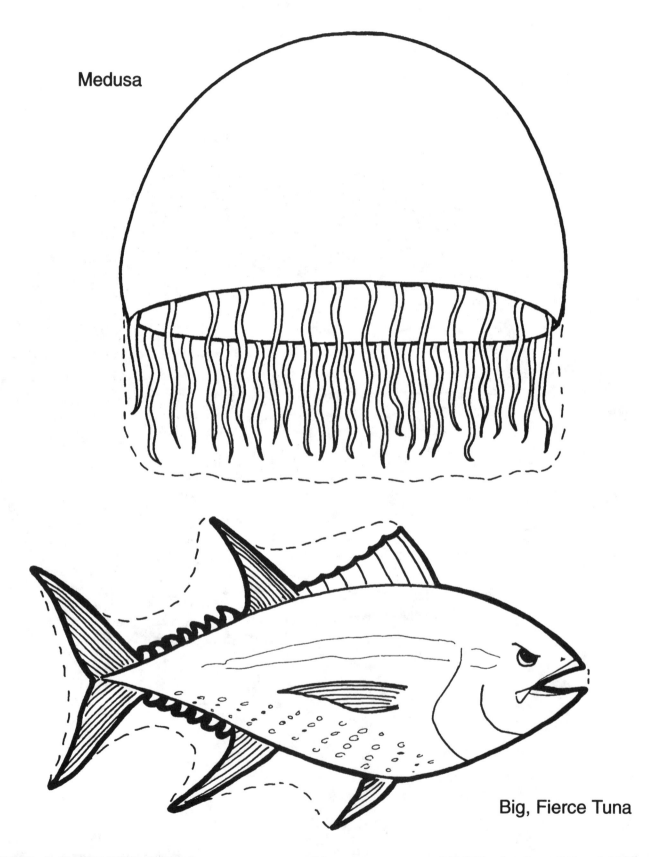

Big, Fierce Tuna

Stick Puppet Patterns *(cont.)*

Sea Anemone

Stick Puppet Patterns *(cont.)*

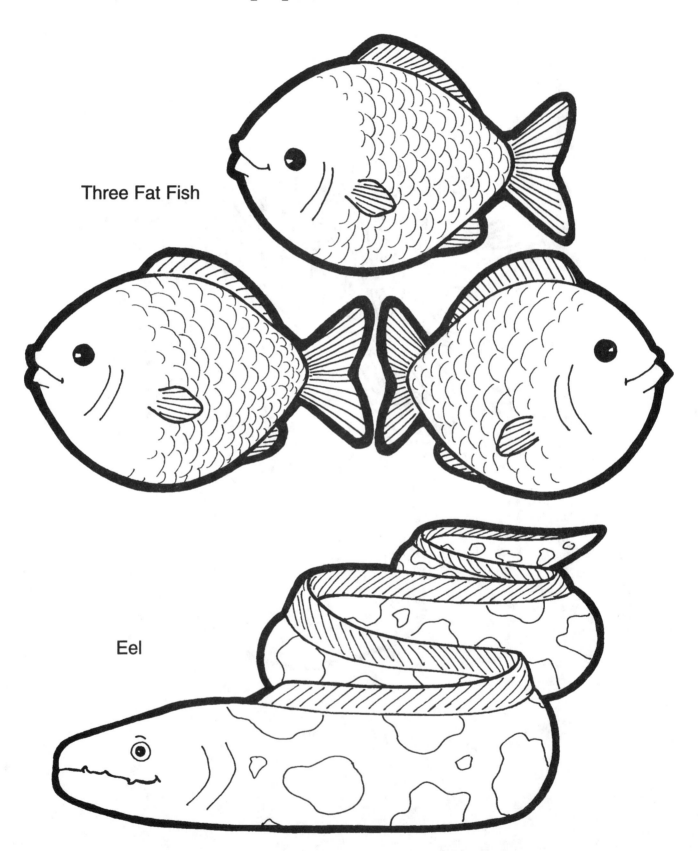

Three Fat Fish

Eel

Stick Puppet Patterns *(cont.)*

Lobster

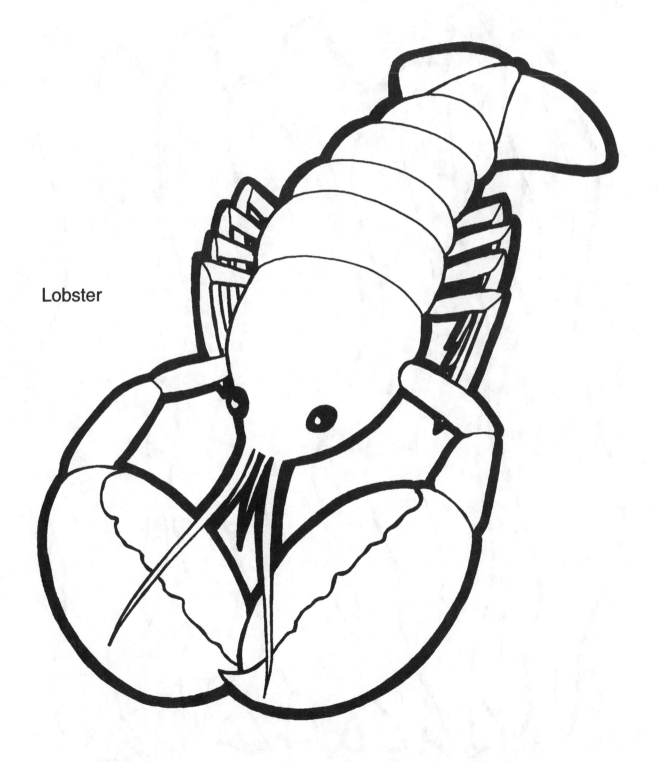

Stick Puppet Patterns (cont.)

Reproduce as many as you need and glue together.

Forest of Seaweed

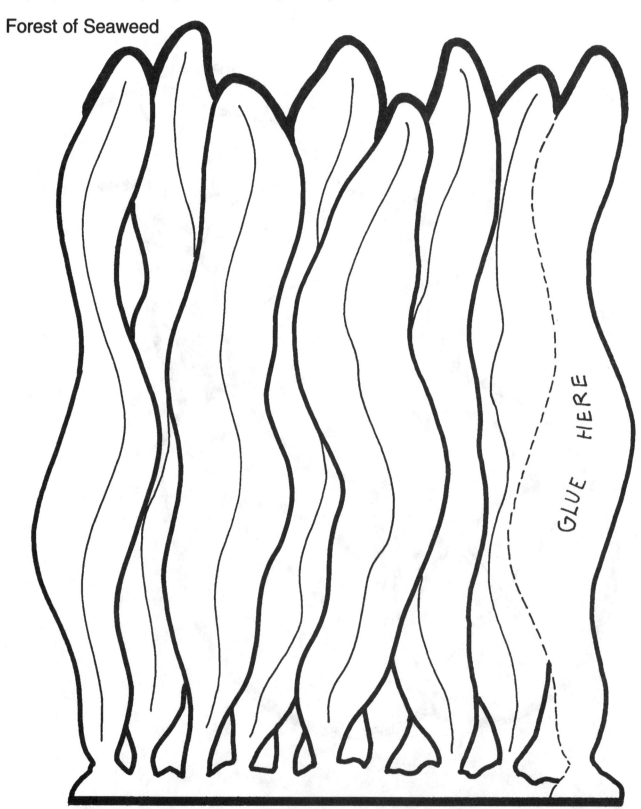

GLUE HERE

94

Fish Kite

You can make a kite that looks like a fish, using the following directions. Have an adult help you.

Materials:

- large paper sack
- stapler
- scissors
- tempera paint
- pieces of sponges

- black construction paper
- streamers
- hole puncher
- string

Directions:

1. Close the corners of the sack and tuck in the ends. Staple.

2. Cut a semicircle from the bottom of the bag for the fish's mouth.

3. Cut two circles from black construction paper. Glue one on each side of the sack as the fish's eyes.

4. Use sponges and tempera paint to make scales on both sides of the sack.

5. Glue streamers onto the bottom of the sack.

6. Punch holes at the top and bottom tips of the mouth.

7. Cut one short and one long piece of string. Tie the short string to the holes you punched in the fish's mouth. Tie the long string to the short string.

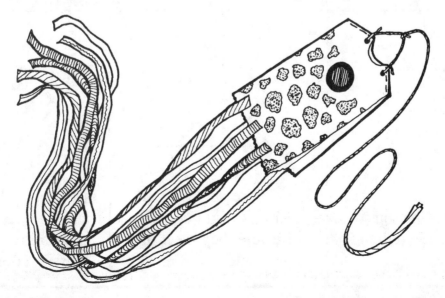

Origami Fish

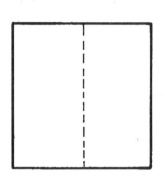

1. Make two rectangles by folding a square piece of paper in half.

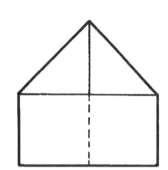

2. Make two triangles by folding down the top corners.

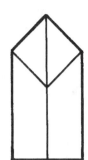

3. Fold in the sides so they meet in the middle.

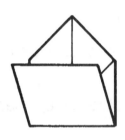

4. Match the bottom edge of the top of the triangles. Fold. Then unfold part way.

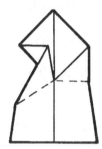

5. Press in the left side.

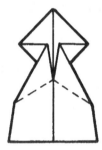

6. Press in the right side.

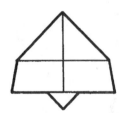

7. Fold down the top so it touches the point at the bottom.

8. Fold the new left and the new right corners. Be sure they meet in the center.

9. Turn the fish over and draw a dot for the eye.

The Frog Prince, Continued

by Jon Scieszka

Summary

The Princess kissed the frog, he turned into a prince and they lived happily ever after, or so the story goes. But the Prince is discontented and goes off into the forest to seek happiness.

Sometimes happiness is found in your own backyard, or your own lily pond.

Extension Activities

Reading Aloud

A good oral language extension activity is to read books aloud related to the subject you are studying. There are many good books about princesses and their problems. Suggestions are listed below. Check in your school or public library for additional titles. Then, use the stories to complete Venn diagrams as described on page 98.

The Paper Bag Princess by Robert N. Munsch
This princess has to rescue her prince from the dragon in a paper bag because the dragon burned up her clothes. It turns out that the prince is not very grateful.

Princess Smartypants by Babette Cole
Princess Smartypants liked her castle and didn't want to get married. Her mother told her to find a husband, so the princess made up some impossible tasks to complete. None of the princes could accomplish these tasks until Prince Swashbuckle came along. He completed them all, so she kissed him and turned him into a toad.

Sleeping Ugly by Jane Yolen
Princess Miserella was beautiful on the outside but ugly on the inside. She stomped off into the forest and met Jane, who was ugly on the outside but beautiful on the inside. The Old Fairy put them all to sleep by mistake, but a poor prince came by and kissed the fairy and Jane but not the princess. So the princess continued to sleep while the rest lived happily ever after.

Prince Cinders by Babette Cole
Prince Cinders has three big, hairy brothers who go to the disco without him. He has to stay home and clean. A fairy, who is not too nice, tries to help. She makes a lot of mistakes, but all's well that ends well.

Snow White in New York by Fiona French
This highly stylized version of Snow White is set in contemporary New York City. The art work is fabulous.

Extension Activities *(cont.)*

Oral Language Organizer: Character Venn Diagram

Draw a Venn diagram on butcher paper or on the chalkboard. Compare the Prince or Princess from *The Frog Prince, Continued* and one other story that the class has read. As a whole class, work on filling in the information by specifying similarities and differences. Use the diagram below as a guide.

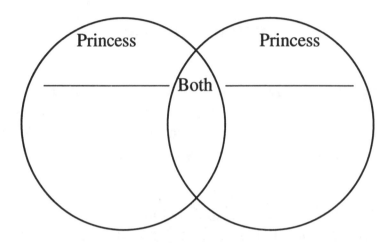

Puppet Show

> **Stage:** Use a tri-fold science presentation board to make the puppet stage. Decorate it like a castle, using the diagram below as a guide. A pattern for the turret is provided (page 99).

> **Puppets:** Use commercial puppets of a frog and a girl dressed as a princess, or make paper bag puppets using the patterns provided (pages 100 and 101).

> **Lighting:** Use an overhead transparency spotlight, as previously described (page 7).

Frog Math

Students work simple addition and subtraction problems to complete this activity (page 103).

Turret Pattern

Paper Bag Princess Pattern

Directions: Cut out the pattern, glue it to a paper bag, and then color.

100

Paper Bag Frog Pattern

Directions: Cut out the pattern, glue it to a paper bag and then, color.

A Conversation with the Princess and the Frog

by Lynn DiDominicis

Characters:	
Princess	Froggie

Princess: Good morning, Froggie. It's so nice to see that you're well.

Froggie: Hey, Princess, sweetheart, what's it to you?

Princess: Now don't mind him. *(to the audience)* He just got up on the wrong side of the pond this morning.

Froggie: Yeah, well how would you like it? A bunch of dumb frogs croakin' all over the place . . .and those nasty mosquitoes are everywhere!

Princess: Why, Froggie, dear . . .do you mean that you miss the FABULOUS meals I was preparing for you with my own little, petite hands?

Froggie: Give me a break—you never made a decent meal in your life. And furthermore . . .

Princess: But, Froggie, my sweet—I took you to so many wonderful places . . .the opera, ballooning . . .

Froggie: I told you, Princess, sweetheart, I wanted to go to the FIGHTS!

Princess: Now, listen, dear sweet little Froggie, all I want to do is turn you into a prince of a fellow. Now give us a kiss.

Froggie: WHAT?!! Are you out of your mind? I'd rather kiss chicken lips!

Princess: Oh, be a dear, Froggie. Just one little kiss!

Froggie: NEVER! You'll have to catch me first!

(Froggie hops away—Princess chases him, then stops to say last line)

Princess: Next time, I'm going to call Acme Royal Dating Service!

Frog Math

Directions: Cut out the frogs. Add or subtract. If the answer is 5, glue the frog in the pond.

103

The Red Balloon

by Albert Lamorisse

Summary

Pascal finds a red balloon but has trouble hanging on to it. Many people try to take his balloon, but he triumphs in the end.

Extension Activities

Movie Viewing

Obtain a copy of the movie *The Red Balloon* and view it together. See the technology bibliography (page 142) for information. This movie can be rented in most video stores.

Balloon Matching

Have students improve visual discrimination by completing a matching activity with pictures of balloons (page 112). You may wish to have students color the balloons red, to match Pascal's.

Mime Production

Have students give a presentation using mime. Directions and script cards are shown below and on pages 105–111.

Staging:

Ceiling net—filled with inflated red balloons

Black background

Top—one helium balloon taped on

Big box—filled with helium balloons

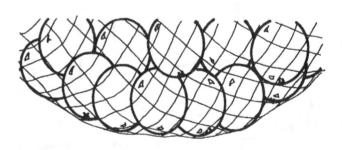

Lighting:

Use a pink transparency with a hole cut out of black paper. Use on an overhead projector.

Black paper

Pink transparency

Costumes:

Pascal: red T-shirt

Five Gang Members: black T-shirts

Five Friends: white T-shirts

Extension Activities *(cont.)*

Props:

One stool

One big box with lid

Chimes or bells

20 red, helium-filled balloons with strings attached

50–70 inflated red balloons (Use more balloons if possible. The effect is better.)

Ceiling net: Use a fish net or plastic net available from a theater supply store.

Music:

Use Antonio Vivaldi's "Concerto for Two Trumpets in C." See the technology bibliography for information (page 142).

Directions:

Each action is done in order. The actions are printed separately to make the events easier to stage. Copy the actions and laminate them, or glue them onto pieces of cardboard. Give each actor his or her action, which is numbered. Then, as you rehearse, call out the numbers so that each actor learns what to do and in what order to do it. These cards can be eliminated as the actors learn their parts.

Mime Script Cards

 1. Pascal enters, finds balloon, takes it, and stands next to box, stage left, looking up.

 2. One gang member sneaks in, back stage right, and breaks balloon from behind with a pin.

Mime Script Cards *(cont.)*

3. **Pascal sits on stool, dejected, head in hands.**

4. **Friend enters, lower stage right, takes one balloon from box, goes to Pascal, and gives it to him, exits stage right.**

5. **Pascal stands next to box, stage left, looking up.**

6. **Gang member sneaks in, grabs balloon, and runs, exiting stage right.**

106

Mime Script Cards *(cont.)*

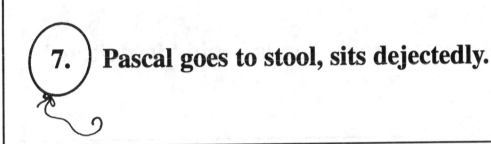

7. Pascal goes to stool, sits dejectedly.

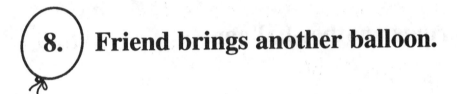

8. Friend brings another balloon.

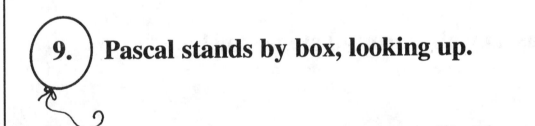

9. Pascal stands by box, looking up.

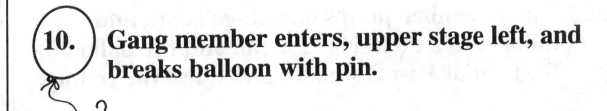

10. Gang member enters, upper stage left, and breaks balloon with pin.

Mime Script Cards *(cont.)*

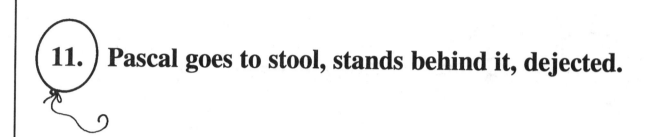
11. Pascal goes to stool, stands behind it, dejected.

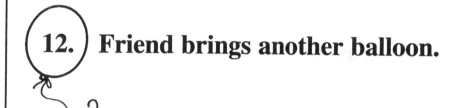
12. Friend brings another balloon.

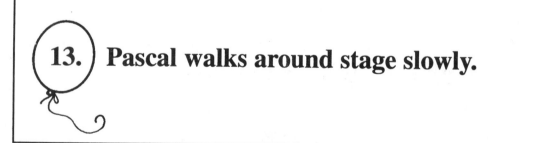
13. Pascal walks around stage slowly.

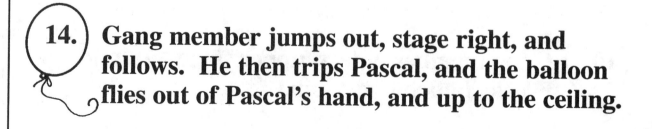
14. Gang member jumps out, stage right, and follows. He then trips Pascal, and the balloon flies out of Pascal's hand, and up to the ceiling.

Mime Script Cards *(cont.)*

 **15.** Pascal crawls to the stool and then sits on the floor in front of it, head in his arms.

 **16.** Friend brings another balloon.

 **17.** Pascal goes to lower stage right and puts his arms around the balloon to protect it.

 **18.** Gang member comes; they slowly wrestle. Then they stand up, face to face. The balloon breaks. (This must look spontaneous—have Pascal hold it at chest level and help it with a pin, using arm away from audience.)

Mime Script Cards *(cont.)*

 **19.** **Pascal runs to lower stage left, sits, and pretends to cry.**

 **20.** **Gang members enter from backstage right and left, tiptoe to back of the box and pretend to get ready to open it and steal balloons.**

 **21.** **Friends crawl in from lower stage right and left towards box.**

 22. **Offstage, bell chimes—everyone freezes. Pascal looks up.**

Mime Script Cards *(cont.)*

 **23.** **Quickly, friends open the box as the ceiling net is overturned, releasing the remaining helium balloon.**

 24. **Gang members fall on floor in a pattern.**

 25. **Pascal goes to center stage, looks up.**

 **26.** **Friends are on knees, across front with back to audience, clapping.**

The Red Balloon by Albert Lamorisse (Doubleday, 1956)

Balloon Matching

Directions: Match the number of balloons.

3 balloons		1 balloons	
5 balloons		8 balloons	
2 balloons		4 balloons	

Cut and paste the balloons into the right boxes above.

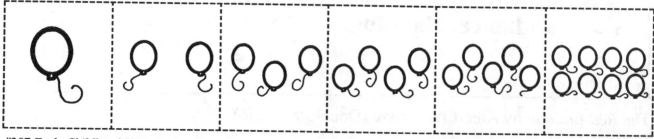

112

"I Am Flying"

by Jack Prelutsky

Summary

Taken from the poetry anthology, The New Kid on the Block *this is a poem that dreams about what it would be like to fly.*

Extension Activities

Who Flies?

Discuss with students what kinds of things can fly. Students responses can include kites, birds, bats, planes, helicopters, rockets, and the space shuttle. Then ask students how these things are alike and how they are different. Lead students to conclude that these things do not use the same method of flying—some have wings, others float in the air, and still others use fuel.

Kites

If possible take students outside on a windy day and have them fly kites. Then cut construction paper into kite shapes and allow students to decorate the paper kites.

Oral Language Organizer: Brainstorm Chart

Ask students to imagine what it would be like to fly. Ask them to brainstorm descriptive words that tell where they are flying, when they are flying, what they see as they fly, and how they are flying. Use the graphic organizer (page 114) to record students' responses. Encourage students to elaborate on their responses, using as many descriptive words as possible. When having students describe how they are flying, you may wish to call their attention to synonyms and antonyms for their responses.

Drama Activity: Response Poetry

Read the poem (page 115) to the class. Using the words on the brainstorm chart as a resource, have the class work in pairs or with the teacher to create poetry responses.

1. Each student takes turns being the reader and the writer. The reader reads a line of the poem, and then the writer (or teacher) writes down whatever comes to mind as students respond to what is said.

2. After each response is written down, it is time to re-read the poem. The reader reads a line of the poem, and the writer reads the response.

Example: (Reader) Fly like a bird? How absurd!

(Response) Soar with wings—surprise a bird!

3. The poem can be changed by reading the response line first and then the line of the poem. The response lines can also stand alone as a new, separate poem.

4. An original poem is provided (page 115) to which students can write their responses.

Graphic Organizer

WHERE

WHEN

FLYING

WHAT

HOW

Fly Like a Bird

by Lynn DiDominicis

Fly Like A Bird? How Absurd!

Arms That Flap Like Wings,

Legs That Do Crazy Things.

How Absurd To Fly Like A Bird.

Wait! What's This? Up In The Air?

Floating So High With The Wind In My Hair.

Fly Like A Bird? Not So Absurd!

Maybe It's Only Absurd To A Bird!

 #207 Early Childhood Units for Drama

I Wish I Were a Butterfly

by James Howe

Summary

A cricket thinks that he is ugly and wishes that he were a butterfly. He meets many other animals who try to explain to him that everyone is beautiful in his or her own way.

Extension Activities

Oral Language Organizer: Character Web

This activity can be used in cooperative groups or as a whole-class activity. Reproduce the web (page 118) for each group or draw it on the chalkboard or on butcher paper. The group leader takes suggestions for character traits for each of the characters, listing them in the web. These can be used as a springboard to develop and discuss the personality of each character. It will be useful in writing script lines for each character.

Stained Glass Butterfly

Have students trace two copies of the butterfly pattern (page 127) onto tagboard. Help them cut out the center parts of the wings and the bodies. Show students how to glue pieces of different colored tissue paper onto one of the patterns. Then have them glue the other pattern on top. Allow the glue to dry. Use string or yarn to hang the butterflies in front of the classroom windows. You may wish to make mobiles using the butterflies.

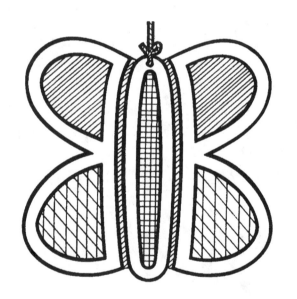

Butterfly Life Cycle

Have students learn about the stages a butterfly goes through during its life. Have them glue the pictures in the appropriate places (page 128). Discuss the pictures and the stages. If possible, keep a caterpillar in your classroom. Allow students to observe the changes.

Extension Activities *(cont.)*

How Much Does a Cricket Eat?

This is a hands-on guided science discovery experience. Students will hypothesize through prediction; they will investigate and then draw conclusions.

Materials:
- one paper cup per student
- one rubber band per student
- plastic wrap to cover each cup
- a large bag of birdseed
- one cotton ball, soaked in water
- one cricket per student, can be obtained at any pet store

Note: Take care not to let the crickets loose in your classroom.

Directions: After the students have looked at the crickets and the birdseed, have each of them guess how much birdseed one cricket will eat in five days. Use the chart provided to keep track of predictions and results.

Have each student (or help each student) place the amount of birdseed they predicted the cricket will eat into a cup and then put the cricket in the cup. Put the cotton ball soaked with water in the cup. Secure the plastic around the top of the cup with a rubber band. Poke some air holes in the plastic wrap with a pin or a nail.

Check the cups each day and replace water if necessary, but do not take the cricket or seeds out.

On the fifth day, carefully collect the crickets in a jar or container, and then have each student count the birdseed that is left.

Chart the results on the chart provided (pages 119 and 120).

Character Web

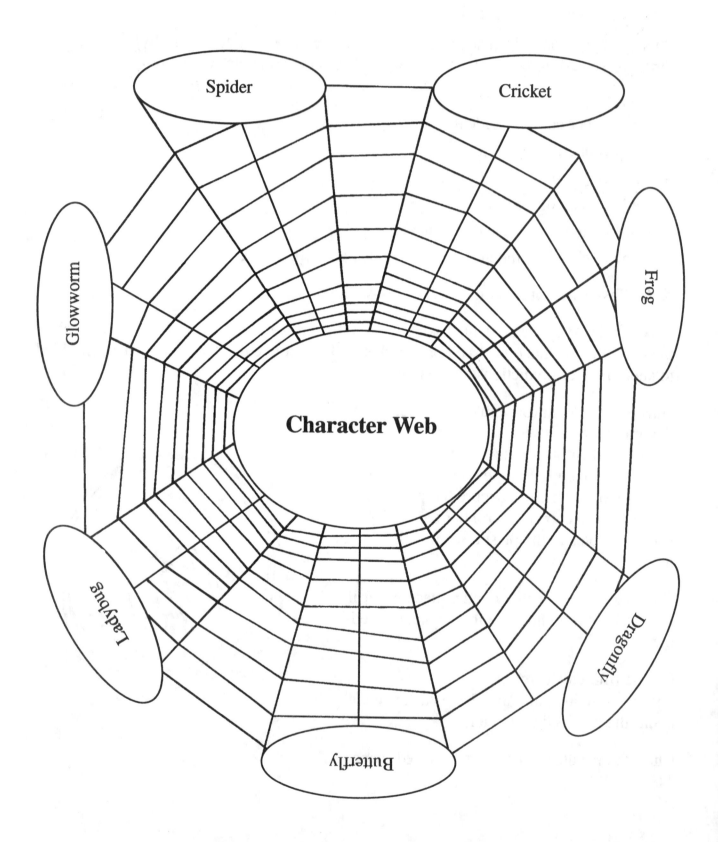

How Much Does a Cricket Eat?

I think my cricket will eat _____birdseeds.
Draw a picture of your cricket in the cup.

Day 1

Day 2

Day 3

How Much Does a Cricket Eat? *(cont.)*

Day 4

Day 5

I predicted my cricket would eat _____ birdseeds.

My cricket really ate _____ birdseeds.

Script Chart

After reading the story and reviewing the character web, you can write your own dialogue to the story. Have each student tell you what each of the characters said to the cricket using their own words. Write it down on the chart. This can be used as the script for the puppet show, or you can use the one provided on page 122.

The Cricket said:

The Glow Worm said:

The Frog said:

The Lady Bug said:

The Dragonfly said:

The Spider said:

The Butterfly said:

Puppet Show

Directions: It will be easier to present this if you pretape the dialogue and background music. Have the music playing in the background. Then have each character record his or her lines using a cassette recorder. This can be played back as the puppeteers perform. Be sure to tape a copy of the script on the inside of the puppet stage so that the puppeteers can follow along. Use picture symbols instead of words for very young students.

Cricket: I can't make music. I wish I were a butterfly. I'm ugly.

Glowworm: Who told you that?

Cricket: The frog said it.

Glowworm: Look at me. I'm no beauty myself.

Cricket: But someday you will be a lightning bug. I wish I were a butterfly.

Ladybug: If I were ugly, I wouldn't care one bit. You must learn to be happy with what you are.

Cricket: That's easy for you to say. I wish I were a butterfly.

Dragonfly: You shouldn't complain. I'm beautiful, and you are, too, in your own way.

Cricket: It's easy to be happy if you're not ugly like me.

Spider: I've been told that I'm ugly.

Cricket: You are not as ugly as I am.

Spider: To me you are beautiful.

Cricket: Then I will play for you as you spin your web.

(Music plays louder as butterflies fly)

Butterfly: What beautiful music! I wish I were a cricket.

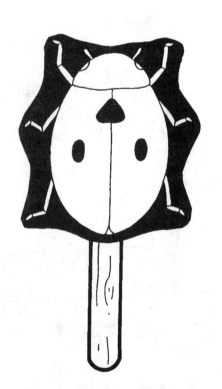

Stick Puppet Patterns

Materials:

- nine craft sticks
- crayons or markers
- neon colored paper
- cardboard
- glitter, if desired
- glue

Directions: Cut out the patterns on pages 123–126. Trace them onto neon colored paper. Then, color and decorate them. Glue them onto pieces of cardboard to make them sturdier. Then glue each one onto a craft stick.

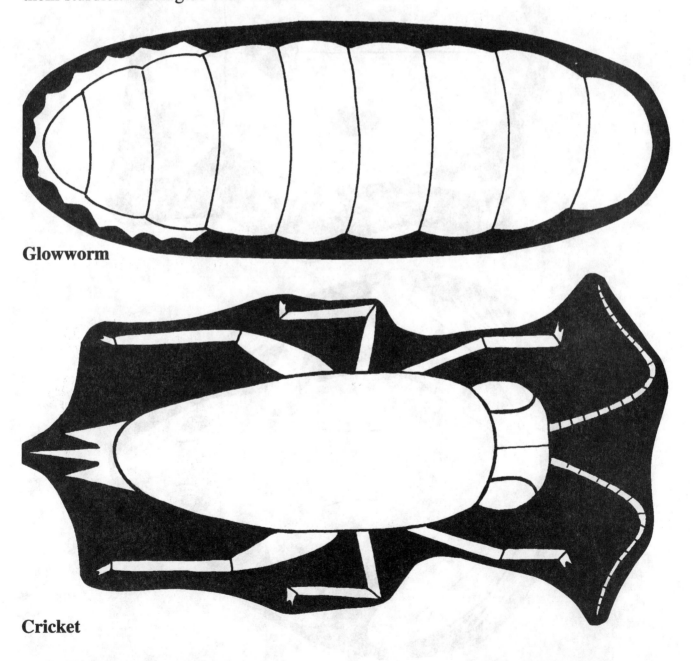

Glowworm

Cricket

Stick Puppet Patterns *(cont.)*

Ladybug

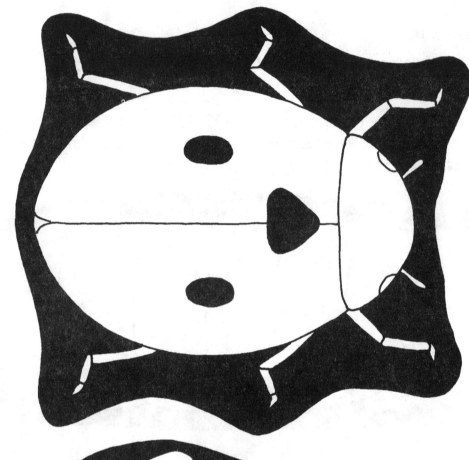

Frog

124

Stick Puppet Patterns (cont.)

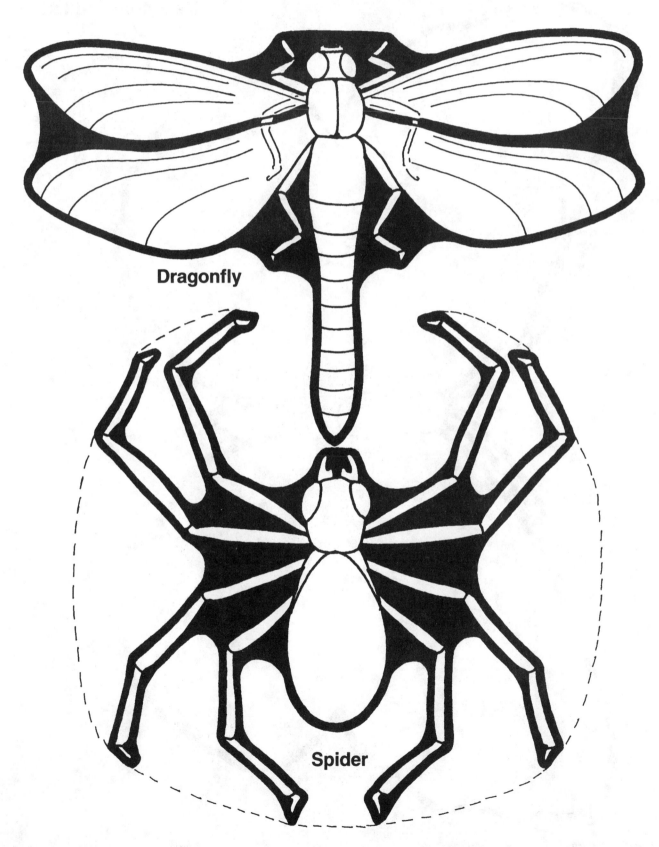

Dragonfly

Spider

Stick Puppet Patterns *(cont.)*

Make three butterflies.

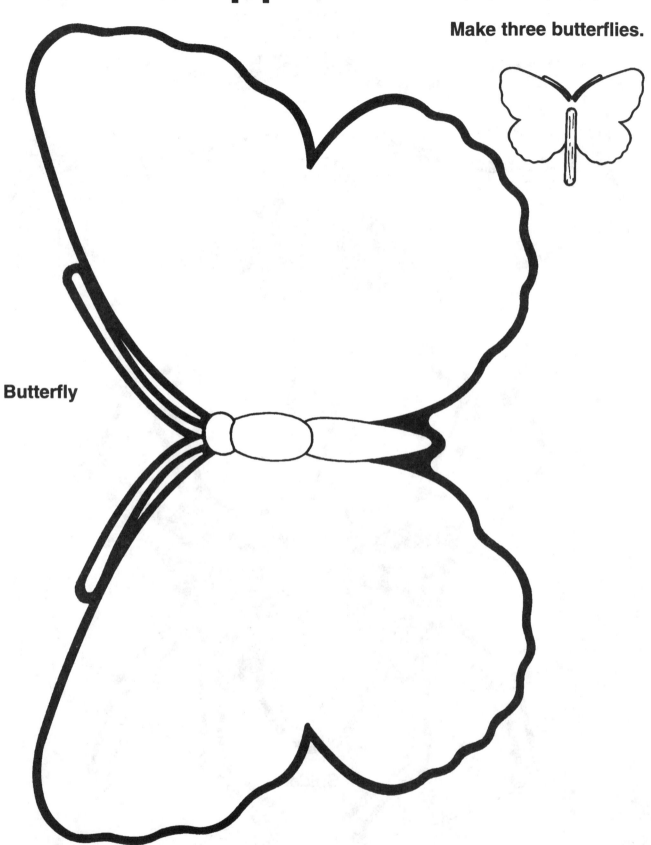

Butterfly

Stained Glass Butterfly Pattern

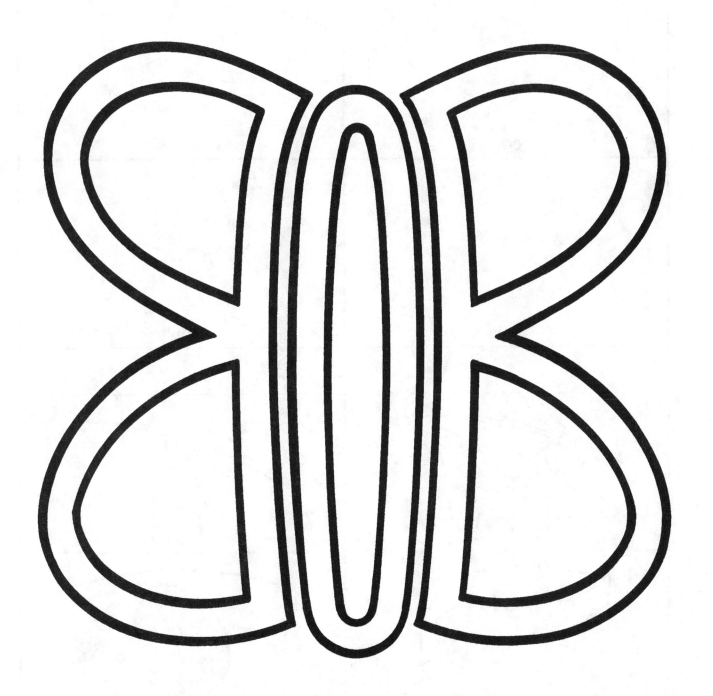

Butterfly Life Cycle

Directions: Glue the pictures in the right order.

egg	caterpillar
pupa	adult

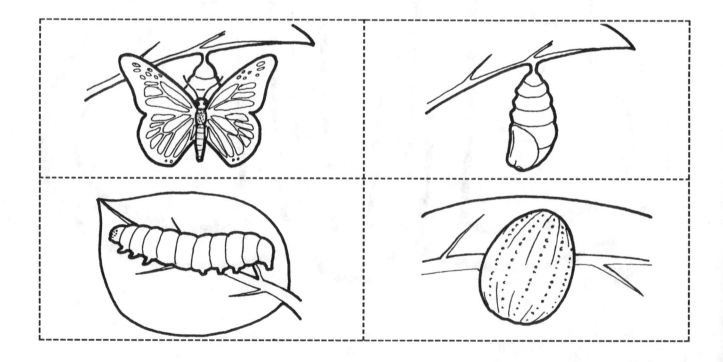

I Know an Old Lady Who Swallowed a Fly

retold and illustrated by Nadine Bernard Westcott

Summary

This is the traditional story of the old lady who swallowed the fly and everything else she swallowed as a result.

Extension Activities

Reading a Book

There are many versions of "I Know an Old Lady Who Swallowed a Fly." Some of them are listed for you in the bibliography (pages 143–144). They are fun to show and read. Ask students to compare/contrast the different versions.

Art Activity

Make an old lady who swallowed a fly from the pattern provided (page 130). Copy enough for the entire class. Have students cut them out and color them. Have students make the pockets from the overlay pattern (page 131). Then have them color and cut out the animals (pages 131–133). Then have students drop the animals into the old lady's "stomach" as you read the story.

Animals

Provide nonfiction books about the different types of animals that the old lady has swallowed. Allow students to examine these books. Read some aloud to the class.

Drama Activity: Song

Sing the song using the traditional tune. Before you sing, you will need to assign three groups.

Group 1: (About half of the class) This group will sing the song, pausing for the other groups to do their sound effects.

Group 2: (About one-fourth of the class) This groups will do the sound effects. They will have to make up a sound effect or action for each animal: fly, spider, bird, cat, dog, goat, cow, horse.

Group 3: This group will repeat the same action every time the words, "Perhaps she'll die" are sung. They will clutch their chests, make groaning noises, fall down, and play dead.

I Know an Old Lady...Patterns

Directions: Glue on the pocket. Then place the animals inside the pocket.

Glue

Glue

Glue

130

I Know an Old Lady...Patterns *(cont.)*

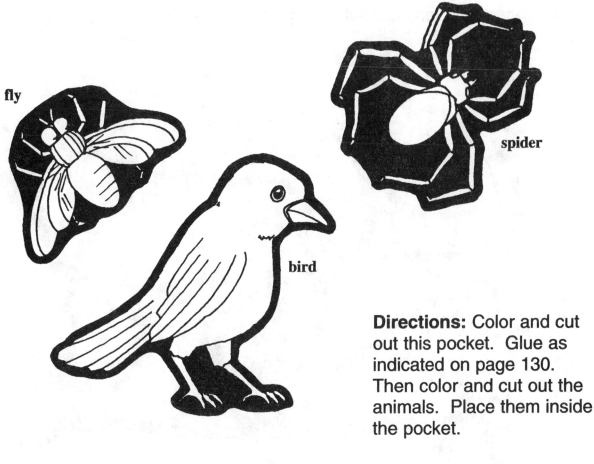

fly

spider

bird

Directions: Color and cut out this pocket. Glue as indicated on page 130. Then color and cut out the animals. Place them inside the pocket.

Pocket

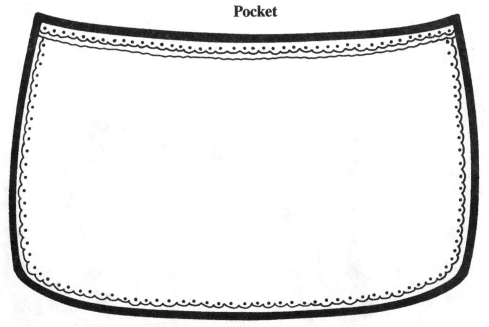

I Know an Old Lady...Patterns (cont.)

Directions: Color and cut out the animals. Place them inside the pocket.

cat

dog

horse

I Know an Old Lady...Patterns (cont.)

Directions: Color and cut out the animals. Place them inside the pocket.

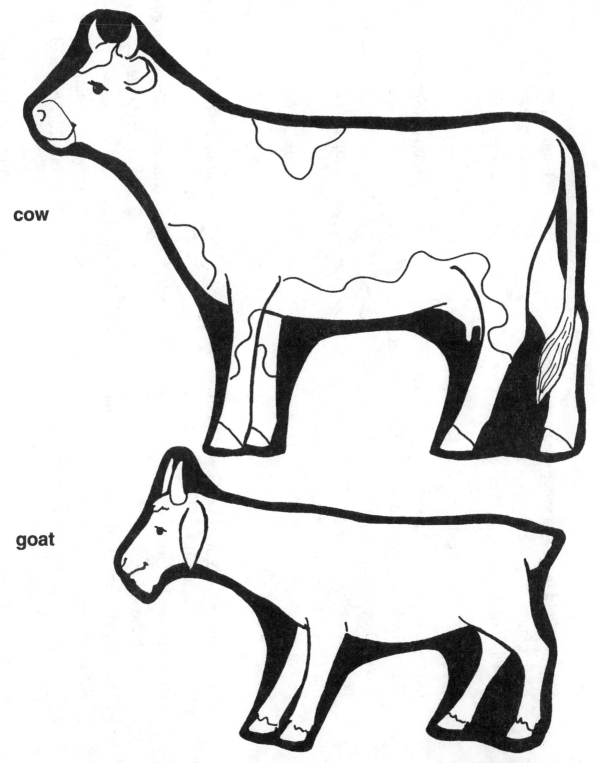

cow

goat

I Know an Old Lady...Song

Group 1:

I know an old lady who swallowed a fly

I don't know why she swallowed a fly

Perhaps she'll die.

Group 2: *(Fly sound)*
Group 2: *(Fly sound)*
Group 3: *(Death scene)*

Group 1:

I know an old lady who swallowed a spider

That wriggled and jiggled and tickled inside her

She swallowed the spider

To catch the fly

But I don't know why she swallowed the fly

Perhaps she'll die.

Group 2: *(Spider action)*

Group 2: *(Spider action)*
Group 2: *(Fly sound effect)*

Group 3: *(Death scene)*

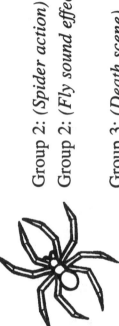

Group 1:

I know an old lady who swallowed a bird

How absurd to swallow a bird.

She swallowed a bird

To catch the spider

That wriggled and jiggled and tickled insider her

She swallowed the spider

To catch the fly

But I don't know why she swallowed the fly

Perhaps she'll die.

Group 2: *(Bird sound effect)*

Group 2: *(Bird sound effect)*
Group 2: *(Spider action)*

Group 2: *(Spider action)*
Group 2: *(Fly sound effect)*

Group 3: *(Death scene)*

I Know an Old Lady...Song *(cont.)*

Group 1:
I know an old lady who swallowed a cat
Imagine that, she swallowed a cat
She swallowed the cat   Group 2: *(Cat sound effect)*
To catch the bird   Group 2: *(Cat sound effect)*
She swallowed the bird   Group 2: *(Bird sound effect)*
To catch the spider   Group 2: *(Bird sound effect)*
   Group 2: *(Spider action)*
That wriggled and jiggled and tickled insider her
She swallowed the spider   Group 2: *(Spider action)*
To catch the fly   Group 2: *(Fly sound effect)*
But I don't know why she swallowed the fly
Perhaps she'll die.   Group 3: *(Death scene)*

Group 1:
I know an old lady who swallowed a dog   Group 2: *(Dog sound effect)*
What a hog to swallow a dog
She swallowed the dog   Group 2: *(Dog sound effect)*
To catch the cat   Group 2: *(Cat sound effect)*
She swallowed the cat   Group 2: *(Cat sound effect)*
To catch the bird   Group 2: *(Bird sound effect)*
She swallowed the bird   Group 2: *(Bird sound effect)*
To catch the spider   Group 2: *(Spider action)*
That wriggled and jiggled and tickled inside her
She swallowed the spider   Group 2: *(Spider action)*
To catch the fly   Group 2: *(Fly sound effect)*
But I don't know why she swallowed the fly
Perhaps she'll die.   Group 3: *(Death scene)*

I Know an Old Lady...Song (cont.)

Group 1:

I know an old lady who swallowed a goat

Just opened her throat and swallowed that goat

She swallowed the goat

To catch the dog

She swallowed the dog

To catch the cat

She swallowed the cat

To catch the bird

She swallowed the bird

To catch the spider

That wriggled and jiggled and tickled inside her

She swallowed the spider

To catch the fly

But I don't know why she swallowed the fly

Perhaps she'll die.

Group 2: *(Goat sound effect)*

Group 2: *(Goat sound effect)*

Group 2: *(Dog sound effect)*

Group 2: *(Dog sound effect)*

Group 2: *(Cat sound effect)*

Group 2: *(Cat sound effect)*

Group 2: *(Bird sound effect)*

Group 2: *(Bird sound effect)*

Group 2: *(Spider action)*

Group 2: *(Spider action)*

Group 2: *(Fly sound effect)*

Group 3: *(Death scene)*

I Know an Old Lady...Song (cont.)

Group 1:

I know an old lady who swallowed a cow

I'll never know how she swallowed a cow

She swallowed a cow   Group 2: (*Cow sound effect*)

To catch the goat   Group 2: (*Cow sound effect*)

She swallowed the goat   Group 2: (*Goat sound effect*)

     Group 2: (*Goat sound effect*)

To catch the dog   Group 2: (*Dog sound effect*)

She swallowed the dog   Group 2: (*Dog sound effect*)

To catch the cat   Group 2: (*Cat sound effect*)

She swallowed the cat   Group 2: (*Cat sound effect*)

To catch the bird   Group 2: (*Bird sound effect*)

She swallowed the bird   Group 2: (*Bird sound effect*)

To catch the spider   Group 2: (*Spider action*)

That wriggled and jiggled and tickled inside her

She swallowed the spider   Group 2: (*Spider action*)

To catch the fly   Group 2: (*Fly sound effect*)

But I don't know why she swallowed the fly

Perhaps she'll die.   Group 3: (*Death scene*)

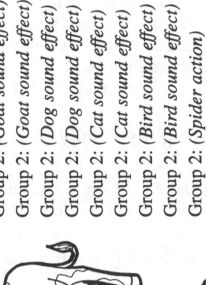

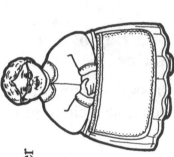

Group 1:

I know an old lady who swallowed a horse   Group 2: (*Horse sound effect*)

Groups 1 and 2:   Group 3:

She died, of course!   (*Final, dramatic death scene*)

An American Thanksgiving— A Pageant

by Lynn DiDominicis

Pageantry: This is a pageant using many people in the cast, appropriately costumed, with props. It needs to be performed on a large stage. It is sung to the tune of "The Twelve Days of Christmas." Each verse has words that should be acted out by the group representing it, and the action is repeated each time it is sung. It has built in confusion and hilarity. The pageant can be performed for a variety of audiences, such as other classes, the parents and family of your students, or as a part of a PTA program.

On The First Day of Thanksgiving My Family Gave to Me—A Football Game for All to See.

A group of students wearing football game attire enter, take their places, and yell "Yeah" every time this line is sung. They should wave flags and pom-poms.

On The Second Day of Thanksgiving My Family Gave to Me—Two Plump Pumpkins . . .

Two students dressed as pumpkins enter and sit down in front of a corn stalk. They should stand each time their verse is sung.

On The Third Day of Thanksgiving My Family Gave to Me—Three Bags of Groceries . . .

Three students enter, staggering under the load of three full bags of groceries. They put them down and pick them up to show the audience each time their verse is sung.

A Pageant *(cont.)*

On The Fourth Day of Thanksgiving My Family Gave to Me—Four Gobbling Turkeys . . .

Have four students dress up as turkeys and have them gobble each time their verse is sung.

On The Fifth Day of Thanksgiving My Family Gave to Me—The Macy's Thanksgiving Day Parade . . .

You will need a minimum of ten students parading across the stage each time this verse is sung. They go back and forth from left to right on each succeeding verse. Some should carry helium balloons. They are led by a drum major with a stick and a whistle. Have some dress in a nursery rhyme costume and be pulled in a wagon like a "float" in a parade. Four to six students should be the marching band, playing rhythm band instruments. See if you can borrow parts of band uniforms from a local high school for costumes. You may wish to have Santa Claus bringing up the rear. Be sure he says, "Ho, Ho, Ho!" each time he enters.

On The Sixth Day of Thanksgiving My Family Gave to Me—Six Potted Mums . . .

Obtain (by purchase or donation) six mum plants. The first time the song is sung, six students carrying the mum plants should enter, then sit in a line across the front of the stage. They will hold up the plants each time their verse is sung.

On The Seventh Day of Thanksgiving My Family Gave to Me—Seven Pies to Bake . . .

Seven "mothers" in aprons enter and take their place as a group. They are carrying bowls. In the bowls are talcum powder and powder puffs. Each time their verse is sung, they take the powder puffs and pat some powder on their faces.

A Pageant *(cont.)*

On The Eighth Day of Thanksgiving My Family Gave to Me—Eight Rooms to Clean . . .

Eight students, armed with brooms, vacuum cleaners, and feather dusters enter. They should be dressed in work clothes, and clean around the actors already on stage. They repeat this each time their verse is sung.

On The Ninth Day of Thanksgiving My Family Gave to Me—Nine Family Portraits . . .

Draw and color nine different "family portraits." Frame them with brown construction paper strips. Have nine students, carrying portraits, enter on their first verse across front of stage, showing portraits to the audience. They then exit and wait for their next march across the front of the stage.

On The Tenth Day of Thanksgiving My Family Gave to Me—Ten Turkey Dinners . . .

This is the centerpiece of this pageant. Have a table set for Thanksgiving in the center of the stage. Ten chairs should be around it. The first time this verse is sung, ten students enter, sit at the table, put pillowcase "napkins" around their necks, hold a knife and a fork upright in each hand and say together, "yum, yum." Then they stay for the next verse.

On The Eleventh Day of Thanksgiving My Family Gave to Me—Eleven Stomach Aches . . .

The ten students at the table stand in place, bend over and say "Ooooo—my stomach hurts!"

On The Twelfth Day of Thanksgiving My Family Gave to Me—Twelve Antacids . . .

Group at table stands, puts fizzy tablets in glasses of water, and sings, ("Plop, plop, fizz, fizz, oh, what a relief it is!"

Theater Award

WE ARE PROUD TO ANNOUNCE THAT

_____

HAS SUCCESSFULLY COMPLETED
OUR DRAMA UNIT!

Teacher

Date

Technology Bibliography

VIDEOS

Arts Abound Series: The Actor. Great Plains National: Affiliated with the University of Nebraska at Lincoln, 1985.

Henson, Jim. *The Frog Prince.* Children's Television Workshop, 1971.

Lamorisse, Albert. *The Red Balloon.* Good Time Theater, 1956.

MUSIC

Raffi. *Baby Beluga.* MCA Records, 1980.
   (Recommended for use with *Swimmy*)

Tchaikovsky, Peter Ilich. "Waltz of the Flowers" from *The Nutcracker Suite.* Sony Music, 1994.
   (Recommended for use with *I Wish I Were a Butterfly*)

Vivaldi, Antonio. "Concerto for Two Trumpets in C" from *Mad About Vivaldi.* Phillips Classic Productions, 1985.
   (Recommended for use with *The Red Balloon*)

SOFTWARE

Butterflies of the World by REMedia. CD-ROM for MAC; Available from Educorp, 7434 Trade Street, San Diego, California, 92121; 1-800-843-9497.

Children's Treasury I by Queue. (Includes *Jack and the Beanstalk* and *The Three Little Pigs*); CD-ROM for MAC and WIN/DOS; Available from Educorp, 7434 Trade Street, San Diego, California, 92121; 1-800-843-9497.

Favorite Fairy Tales by Queue. (Includes *The Frog Prince*); CD-ROM for MAC and WIN/DOS; Available from Educorp, 7434 Trade Street, San Diego, California, 92121; 1-800-843-9497.

The New Kid on the Block by Broderbund. (Poems by Jack Prelutsky); CD-ROM for MAC/MPC; Available from Educorp, 7434 Trade Street, San Diego, California, 92121; 1-800-843-9497.

The Paper Bag Princess by Discis. CD-ROM for MAC/WIN/DOS; Available from Educorp, 7434 Trade Street, San Diego, California, 92121; 1-800-843-9497.

P.B. Bear's Birthday Party by Dorling Kindersley, Inc. CD-ROM for MAC and MPC; Available from Educorp, 7434 Trade Street, San Diego, California, 92121; 1-800-843-9497.

Reading Development Library Level 1 by The Learning Company. (Includes *Goldilocks and the Three Bears* and *The Three Little Pigs*); CD-ROM for MAC and WIN; Available from Educorp, 7434 Trade Street, San Diego, California, 92121; 1-800-843-9497.

Bibliography

BOOKS RECOMMENDED FOR THIS UNIT (In Order of Appearance)

Kennedy, Jimmy. *The Teddy Bear's Picnic.* Holt, 1992.

Numeroff, Laura Joffe. *If You Give a Mouse a Cookie.* Harper, 1985.

Brett, Jan. *Goldilocks and the Three Bears.* Putnam, 1987.

Marshall, James. *Goldilocks and the Three Bears.* Dial Books for Young Readers, 1988.

Riordan, James. "Jack and the Beanstalk" from *Fairy Tales.* Octopus Books, 1990.

The Three Little Pigs (Big Book). Teacher Created Materials #551, 1992.

dePaola, Tomie. "The Three Billy Goats Gruff" from *Tomie dePaola's Favorite Nursery Rhymes.* Putnam, 1986.

dePaola, Tomie. *Tomie dePaola's Mother Goose.* Putnam, 1985.

Lionni, Leo. *Swimmy.* Alfred A. Knopf, 1963.

Scieszka, Jon. *The Frog Prince, Continued.* Viking, 1991.

Lamorisse, Albert. *The Red Balloon.* Doubleday, 1956.

Prelutsky, Jack. "I Am Flying" from *The New Kid on the Block.* Greenwillow, 1984.

Howe, James. *I Wish I Were a Butterfly.* Harcourt, 1987.

Westcott, Nadine Bernard. *I Know an Old Lady Who Swallowed a Fly.* Little, Brown, 1980.

BEAR BOOKS

Asch, Frank. *Bear Shadow.* Little Simon, 1985.

Bond, Michael. *A Bear Called Paddington.* Dell Yearling Book, 1958.

Freeman, Don. *Corduroy.* Viking Penguin, Puffin Books, 1968.

Hague, Michael. *Teddy Bear, Teddy Bear: A Classic Action Rhyme.* Morrow, 1993.

MOUSE BOOKS

Hoff, Syd. *Mrs. Brice's Mice.* Harper, 1988.

Ivimey, John W. *Three Blind Mice.* Putnam, 1991.

McKissack, Pat. *Country Mouse and City Mouse.* Childrens Press, 1985.

PIG BOOKS

Enderle, Judith Ross and Stephanie Gordon Tessler. *A Pile of Pigs.* Bell Books, 1993.

Retan, Walter. *Piggies Piggies Piggies.* Simon & Schuster, 1993.

Teague, Mark. *Pigsty.* Scholastic, 1994.

Wood, Audrey and Don. *Piggies.* Harcourt Brace Jovanovich, 1991.

Yolen, Jane. *Picnic with Piggins.* Harcourt Brace Jovanovich, 1988.

GOAT/TROLL BOOKS

Blood, Charles. *The Goat in the Rug.* Four Winds Press, 1990.

Jewell, Nancy. *Two Silly Trolls.* Harper, 1992.

Wildsmith, Brian. *Goat's Trail.* Alfred A. Knopf, 1986.

Bibliography (cont.)

FISH BOOKS

Dickens, Lucy. *Go Fish.* Viking, 1991.
Kroll, Steven. *Gone Fishing.* Crown, 1990.
Oppenheim, Joanne. *Follow That Fish.* Bantam, 1990.

PRINCESS BOOKS

Cole, Babette. *Princess Smartypants.* Putnam, 1986.
French, Fiona. *Snow White in New York City.* Oxford University Press, 1986.
Munsch, Robert N. *The Paper Bag Princess.* Annick Press, 1994.

BALLOON/FLYING BOOKS

Crews, Donald. *Flying.* Greenwillow, 1986.
Gibbons, Gail. *Flying.* Holiday, 1986.
Gray, Nigel. *Balloon for Grandad.* Orchard, 1988.

BUTTERFLY BOOKS

Braithwaite, Althea. *Butterflies.* Dearborne, 1988.
Florian, Douglas. *Discovering Butterflies.* Macmillan, 1990.
Mitchell, Victor. *Butterflies.* (Coloring Books). Lion USA, 1988.

I KNOW AN OLD LADY WHO SWALLOWED A FLY BOOKS

Bantock, Nick. *There Was an Old Lady.* Viking Penguin, 1990.
Hawkins, Colin and Jacqi. *I Know an Old Lady Who Swallowed a Fly.* Holiday House, 1990.
Pienkowsdki, Jan. *Oh My a Fly!* Price Stern Sloan, 1989.
Rounds, Glen. *I Know an Old Lady Who Swallowed a Fly.* Holiday House, 1990.

THEATER RESOURCES

Bellville, Cheryl Walsh. *Theater Magic.* Carolrhoda, 1986.
Cook, Wayne D. *Center Stage.* Dale Seymour, 1993.
Renfro, Nancy. *Puppet Shows Made Easy!* Renfro Paper, 1984.

TEACHER CREATED MATERIALS

TCM-182 *Happy Hats: Animals*
TCM-246 *Fairy Tales*
TCM-253 *Community Workers*
TCM-267 *Bears*
TCM-301 *Literature Activities for Young Children*
TCM-302 *Literature Activities for Young Children*
TCM-550 *The Three Bears* (Big Book)
TCM-551 *The Three Little Pigs* (Big Book)
TCM-610 *Hands-On Minds-On Science: Animals*
TCM-615 *Multicultural Holidays*